Lanterns
That Lit Our World
Book Two

Lanterns
That Lit Our World
Book Two

Old Railroad,
Marine, Fire,
Carriage,
Farm & Other
Lanterns

ANTHONY HOBSON

Third Printing, December, 1998

Library of Congress Catalog Card Number: 96-80000
    ISBN: 1-889029-00-9

Published in the United States of America by
    Golden Hill Press, Inc., Spencertown, New York 12165
This book was set in Goudy Old Style
    by Kath Moran of North Wing Studios, Stuart, Florida

Once again, to Cathy, my wife and friend,
who with patience, gives help and love.

Table of Contents

Preface

I wish to thank all my readers for their interest, which contributed so to the success of my first book in this series on American lanterns and their manufacturers. It became apparent to me, with the extensive mail inquiries I have received since its publication, that there is a large and expanding interest in collecting lanterns of diversified styles and manufacture. Not only has your interest encouraged me in the research and writing of this second volume, but various pieces of information which you have sent have helped me better interpret some of my material. Please know that I enjoy hearing from you and do try to answer your inquiries. (And, of course, it would be appreciated if you sent stamped, self-addressed envelopes with them!)

I present this, Book Two, with the purpose of expanding further the available information about old lanterns, and in the hope that it brings you as much pleasure in the reading as it did me in the researching and writing.

As in the first book, I have indicated the original appearance of specific lanterns and their structure, uses, age, rarity and general price range. In the case of pressurized-fuel lanterns, which were not covered in the first volume, I have indicated their workings and evolution. I have also included here the many dead-flame marine lanterns of the period. There has been only fragmented historical material available on these two types of lanterns. I now am able to provide a more coherent body of information on them.

To avoid repetition, I have presented only new material in this present volume. Therefore, I have not repeated the sections of my first volume dealing with lantern parts, workings and history for dead-flame, hot-blast and cold-blast lanterns, and lantern manufacturers noted in the first volume are mentioned here only when I had more material available, or in connection with another manufacturer newly-covered here. I have included some new material on wicks, oil cans and specific burners.

To my mind, the great thing about lantern collecting is that we are not all looking for the same thing. In fact, many of us started by buying a single lantern just because something about it appealed to us: we were not looking for any thing in particular. Of course, as we buy a few more, we usually begin to specialize: in a time period, or a type of lantern, such as hot blast; or in lanterns burning only a particular kind of fuel or having a different kind of globe. The diversification of style within each group is what makes the hobby so interesting. And, of course, the hours of fun spent looking for a rare find — and finding it! I wish you luck in your hunting.

Anthony Hobson
Ghent, New York
August, 1996

Acknowledgments

I cannot express enough appreciation to Herbert Ebendorf, of the Coleman Museum in Wichita, Kansas. He generously shared with me — through communication and correspondence — a great deal of information he had documented on Coleman history and Coleman lanterns. Without his assistance the chapter on Coleman lanterns would not have materialized.

A special thanks to Frederick M. Perkins, Corporate Secretary of Perko, Inc. and great-grandson of the founder of Perkins Marine and Lamp Corporation, who took time from his busy work schedule to look at early company records and supply me with material from those records. Included in my appreciation is Lynda Sykes, from the corporate office of Perko, Inc., who always found time to provide me with photocopies of original catalogues and historical material from Perko company archives.

My thanks also to the many people who made available to me information, photographs and drawings. These include: Alexander C. Black, Douglas, Arizona; Frederick Braun, Pennsylvania; William Courter, Aladdin Knights of the Mystic Light, Kevil, Kentucky; Gerald Fox, Essex Junction, Vermont; Adrian Hurd, Conway, New Hampshire; Robert Nichols, Ashville, New York; and George Vandercook, Lansing, Michigan.

And to Stanley Engel, Ghent, New York, who spent many hours improving drawings that I originally thought were not reproducible. And to the librarians who located information from their collections and made it available to me: Debra Randolf, Reference Librarian, The New-York Historical Society, New York City; Robert G. Robles, Historical Research Librarian, Bristol Public Library, Bristol Connecticut; and Mrs. Noel VanGorden, Detroit Public Library, Detroit, Michigan.

To these, and to all the other people along the way who contributed in large or small ways, I express my thanks. Finally, to my Editor, Mary Zander, thank you for your patience and perseverance in applying your expertise to this manuscript.

American Lanterns: An Overview

Portable, fuel-burning lanterns were indispensable to American life— its transportation, farming, commerce, recreation, and industry, on land and on sea — from Colonial times to the early 20th century. By their light, our nation and our industries, commerce and technologies evolved and grew, and lanterns themselves became more efficient as their styles were modified and refined to fit their expanding uses.

In the early and mid-19th century, lanterns underwent major changes in structure and style as they evolved from primitive metal candleboxes to the more and more efficient dead-flame, and hot- and cold-blast tubular lanterns, which used wicks to burn fuel. In the early 20th century, a major change in lantern technology was the development of lamps using mantles to create better light, and their subsequent refinement and evolution to the gas-pressure or gas-vapor lantern, which used a generator to pressurize the fuel and burn it.

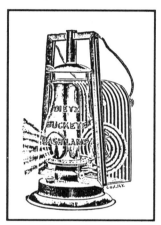

Carriage lantern

Once the various lantern designs — dead-flame, hot- and cold-blast—were set, late in the 19th century, there was constant improvement: new styles of burners; improved air flow within the lantern; new globe designs. Many specialized designs were produced, aimed at new, emerging markets. Some were obvious to the general public, others less so. For example, the lanterns used on then-new automobiles had a specific design of their own. That design grew out of the lanterns used for horse-drawn carriages, but due to the faster speed of the automobile, they needed to be more weatherproof.

Auto lantern

Old style marine lantern

New style marine lantern

Marine lantern design also changed somewhat, becoming more standardized in the early 20th century. This was a direct result of federal regulations issued in 1910 governing ship lighting. These dictated the size of the lens installed in the lantern, and the size of ship they could be used on. In order to comply with these federal marine laws, manufacturers designed new styles of water-and rust-proof lanterns. Many of these are somewhat different in style from other dead-flame lanterns, and most are easily recognized by their Fresnel lenses and their metal, which is mainly brass or copper, highly polished. Galvanized versions can be found, but they lack the deep color and beauty of their brass and copper counterparts.

As the public continued to demand brighter outdoor lights, inventors investigated other light-producing technologies. A major discovery was the Welsbach mantle. When sprayed with a fine mist of combustible fuel such as kerosene or gasoline, this mantle burned with a bright glow. This simple mantle was the catalyst needed to initiate a surge of inventions utilizing its bright light. It evolved to the gas-vapor lantern, using pressurized fuel. Unlike wick-burning lanterns, which had a light output of between two and forty candlepower, these lanterns were capable of producing up to 600 candlepower with a comparably sized lantern. The public was slow to accept the lanterns because they were so much brighter than those customarily used. Pressurized-fuel lanterns, like their wick-burning cousins, also have endless versions and varieties and a distinctive style of design.

Gas-pressure lantern

During the past century and a half, there have been many lantern manufacturers and distributors. Some long-time manufacturers of wick-burning lanterns eventually sold out to other companies or went out of business, while others, such as Dietz, Adlake, and Perkins, solidified their positions. With the advent of pressurized-fuel lanterns some companies attempted to make the transition to manufacturing this new product, but not all succeeded. The Coleman Company eventually emerged as the prime manufacturer and distributor of these gas-pressure lanterns.

Fuel-burning lanterns continued in use well into the 20th century, when they were slowly supplanted by other forms of lighting. Today only one style, the pressurized-fuel lantern, is widely used, primarily for camping and other outdoor recreation. Now, at the end of the 20th century, wick-burning lanterns are no longer manufactured in the United States. The very rural countries that still require wick-burning lanterns purchase them from Japan and Germany. Even these are now in little demand. Apart from some functionally decorative lanterns sold as ornamental lighting, wick-burning lanterns will soon be an historic oddity found only in collections and museums.

Manufacturers/Distributors
Noted in This Book

Acorn Brass Manufacturing Co.	1900-1925	May also have operated as the Chicago Solar Light Co.
Adams & Westlake	1857-Present	
Akron Lamp & Manufacturing Co.	1898-1949	Went out of business.
Alter Light Co.	Early 1900s	Manufactured inverted mantles; later purchased by General Electric.
American Gas Machine Co.	1895-1968	In 1940 became part of Queen Stove Works, but still operated as American Gas Machine until 1968.
American Lamp and Brass Co.; American Lamp Works	1890-1913	Name changed to American Lamp Works, 1905; then merged with National Marine Lamp Co., 1913.
Angle Lamp Co.	1890-1920	Went out of business.
Best Street Light Co.	ca.1875-1915	Went out of business.
Boesch Lamp Co.	1869-1920	Went out of business.
Bristol Brass Co., Lantern Division	1868-1912	Division purchased in 1912 by National Marine Lamp Co.
Buhl Stamping Co.; Buhl Manufacturing Co.	1888-1956	Became Buhl Manufacturing Co. in 1944; closed in 1956.
Chicago Solar Light Co.	1900-1925	See Acorn Brass Co.

Coleman Lamp Co.; Coleman Co., Inc.	1899-Present	Started in 1899 as Hydro-Carbon Light Co.; in 1913 became Coleman Lamp Co.; later, Coleman Co., Inc.
Defiance Lantern & Stamping Co.	1900-1935	Also manufactured Rayo-marked lanterns. Bought by Embury Mfg. Co.
R.E. Dietz Co.	1869-1992	Ceased manufacturing in U.S.; overseas-manufactured lanterns still available from Dietz sales department.
Dressel Railway Lamp & Signal Co.	1882-1920s	Merged with F.H. Lovell Co.
Charles Durkee and Co.	1903-1920s	Went out of business.
Economy Gas Light Co.; Economy Gas Lamp Co.	1898-1926	Went out of business.
Robert Findlay Manufacturing Co.	ca.1910-1924	Ceased manufacturing in 1921; maintained sales office until 1924.
Forestville Marine Lamp Co.	1932-1937	A reorganization of National Marine Lamp Co.; went out of business.
C.T. Ham Manufacturing Co.	1886-1914	Closed in 1914; bought by Dietz in 1915; many Ham designs found in Dietz line thereafter.
H. A. J. Helvig Co.	1879-1906	In 1906 reorganized as the National Marine Lamp Co., a distributor, and later, manufacturer.
Howard and Morse Co.	1867-1898	Went out of business.
Hurwood Manufacturing Co.; John A. Hurley, Inc.	1903-1915	In 1909 name changed to John A. Hurley; went out of business.
Hydro-Carbon Light Co. (See Coleman.)	1899-1913	Name changed in 1913 to Coleman Co.
Incandescent Light & Supply Co.	1900-1914	Acquired by Coleman in 1914.

J.H. Kelly Co.	1856-1897	From 1871-1876, C.T. Ham was a partner in this company
Keystone Lantern Co.	1903-1930	Went out of business.
F.H. Lovell & Co.; Lovell-Dressel	1864-1968	Name changed in early1920s when bought Dressel Railway Lamp and Signal Co.; bought by Adlake in 1968.
Manhattan Brass Co.	1868-1914	Went out of business.
Mantle Lamp Co.	Early 1900s-1960	Manufactured Aladdin table lamps.
Edward Miller & Sons	1890s (?)-1910s(?)	Manufactured Rayo and Efficient lamps and some lanterns.
Nagel-Chase Manufacturing Co.	1904- ca. 1930	Went out of business.
National Marine Lamp Co.	1906-1930	H.A.J. Helvig reorganized as a distributor, 1906; became manufacturer, 1912; reorganized as Forestville Marine Lamp Co.,1932; went out of business.
Pennsylvania Globe Gas Lighting Co.	?	In 1899 got manufacturing rights for hanging mantle.
F. Persky & Co.; Persky & Sumergrade; Perkins Marine Lamp and Hardware Corp.; Perko, Inc.	1901-Present	In 1904, changed to Persky & Sumergrade; in 1910 to Perkins Marine; in 1961 to Perko.
Pitner Gasoline Lighting Co.	1902-1915	Went out of business.
Porter Co.; Wm. Porter & Son; Wm. Porter's Sons	1862-1922	In 1868 named changed to Wm. Porter & Sons; in 1903 to Wm. Porter's Sons; ceased manufacturing in 1909; maintained sales office until 1922.
Prentiss Waber Product Co.; Preway, Inc.	1915-1980s	After 1952 name changed to Preway, Inc.
Socony Petroleum Products Division		A sales division of Standard Oil Company; sold Rayo lanterns 1906-ca. 1924.

Sears, Roebuck	1890-Present	
Steam Gauge & Lantern Co.	1881-1897	Bought by R.E. Dietz.
Sunshine Safety Lamp Co.	1910-1928	Merged into Coleman Lamp Co. in 1928.
Thomas Manufacturing Co.	1908-1926	Went out of business.
Nathaniel Tufts Co.; Tufts Brothers	1879-1902	Became Tufts Bros. in 1893.
Universal Metal Spinning & Stamping Co.	ca. 1910-1922	Went out of business.
Joseph Vogel	1884-1912	Went out of business.
Montgomery Ward Co.	1872-Present	
Welsbach Commercial Co.; Welsbach Co.	1890-?	Division of United Gas Improvement Co. established to manufacture mantles.
Westinghouse Lamp Co.; Westinghouse; WCI Corp.	1901-Present	Bought all Welsbach patents and manufactured the lamps beginning in 1906.
Wilcox, Crittenden, & Co; North & Judd Manufacturing Co.	1847-Present	
Yale Light Co.	?-1914	Merged with the Coleman Co. in 1914.

Section I
Wick-Burning Lanterns: Railroad, Fire, Industry, Farm, Carriage

PRICE LIST

OF

—SPENCER'S PATENT—

TWO LIGHT

Student Lamps.

"HURRICANE,"

"Storm," I X L and Woodward,

ALL BRASS,

LANTERNS, &c.

MANUFACTURED BY

MANHATTAN BRASS CO.,

Office, 83 Reade Street,

Works, 1st Ave., 27th & 28th Sts.,   NEW YORK.

Early catalogue cover for Manhattan Brass Company.

Manhattan Brass Company

Operating from 1868 to 1914, Manhattan Brass Company had a large manufacturing factory in New York City on First Avenue between Twenty-seventh and Twenty-eighth Streets. They retailed brass items — including kerosene lamps and lanterns — out of their store and head office at 83 Reade Street. Their main business, however, was to wholesale to other manufacturers and distributors. These included large companies such as Plume & Atwood, Edward Miller and Sons Company, and Sears, Roebuck. During 1907 Manhattan Brass manufactured, for Standard Oil Company, a quantity of table lamps marked "Rayo."

Most of Manhattan's products were not marked, but many of their lanterns and lamps are easily recognized by the unique dark and light bands on the brass fonts, as shown in this example.

Example of the dark and light coloring found on brass lanterns and lamps of this company.

Hurricane
1868 – 1880

Sizes 1, 2, and 3 were advertised.
Finish: all brass.
Wire or chain bail available.

Very rare.

Storm
1874 – 1890

Finish: all brass.

Very rare.

Woodward

1868 – 1885

Finish: all brass.

Very rare.

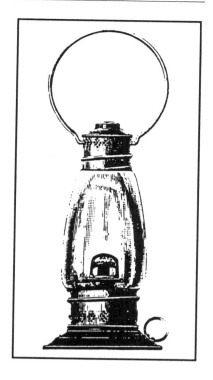

Buhl Stamping Company's Works, c. 1890.

The Burn Brothers, Walter and William.

Buhl Stamping Company

This diversified company was established in the spring of 1888 with capital of $75,000. Theodore D. Buhl was president, Walter S. Burn, treasurer and manager, and his brother, William H. Burn, secretary. The Burn brothers were born and educated in Toronto, and learned the sheet metal and lantern business from two of the leading hardware concerns in Montreal. Theodore Buhl was born in Detroit on August 20, 1844, and died in 1907. He was educated at home and in New Haven, Connecticut. Immediately after his schooling ended he went to work at Buhl, Sons and Company, a large and well-established Detroit wholesale hardware business owned by his father.

In 1888, in partnership with the Burn brothers, Theodore Buhl established the Buhl Stamping Company in the city block bounded by Third and Fourth Streets, and Larned and Congress Streets. This property was originally owned by the Detroit Copper Brass Rolling Mill. City records that year indicate that Buhl, Sons and Company owned the vacant buildings on this site. Buhl employed between 150 and 160 people to manufacture its main product — milk cans and milk containers — producing about 20,000 per month in sizes from one to ten gallons. These were used to ship milk by railroad all over the United States. Circular saws, cross cut saws, and sheet metal wares were also produced.

Another large portion of the factory was devoted to the manufacture of tubular —hot- and cold-blast — lanterns, lamps, and brass burners. In 1891 the Detroit Record of Commerce lists Buhl as having the capacity to produce 250 tubular lanterns daily. Their tubular lanterns were sold through hardware stores and dairy supply houses. At the Lantern Association annual meeting on January 13, 1892, Buhl reported prior-year sales as 5,290 dozen tubular lanterns. The years 1895 to 1899 showed an average yearly sale of 6,000 dozen tubular lanterns.

Other records indicate that dead-flame railroad-style lanterns were also produced by Buhl from 1888 until around 1896. It is likely that Buhl still manufactured limited quantities of dead-flame lanterns after this date, but by then the company concentrated their lantern manufacturing on tubular lanterns, as farms and rural areas were their main market. They were still manufacturing lanterns between the two World Wars, and up to 1930 list lanterns in their catalogue.

During the First and Second World Wars Buhl Stamping Company played an important part in war production, and in 1944 changed its name to the Buhl Manufacturing Company, to fit its more diversified product line. From 1945 to 1956 the Buhl address was 2730 Scotten Street in Detroit. After 1956 the company is no longer listed in the city directories or telephone books.

Buhl lanterns are marked "Buhl" on their tops or fonts. Prior to 1913 they were given model numbers. After this date Buhl brought out a new line referred to as "Royal" tubular lanterns. They were given names such as "Daisy" or "Majestic," clearly marked on the font. Many of the named models were identical to the numbered models manufactured prior to 1913. In the following pages the new name as well as the old model (1888-1912) numbers are given wherever known.

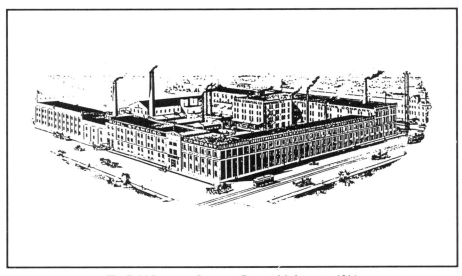

The Buhl Stamping Company, Detroit, Michigan, in 1914.

No. 10
1888 – 1913

No. 1 burner, 5/8" wick; 1 pint font.
Hot blast.
No. O globe, available in clear, or red.
Finish: bright tin, both models.
The wick was lit via a sliding door in the globe base.

From 1913 – 1930 this model had a domed font and was called the **Daisy.**

Rare.

Princess
1913 – 1930

No. 2 burner, 1" wick.
Hot blast.
No. 0 globe, available in clear only with this lantern. Colored globes were special order.
Finish: bright tin.

There were some pre-1913 models. They had flat-top fonts.

Common.

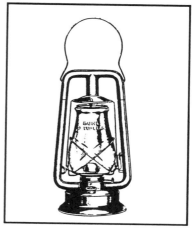

Side Wall Reflector
1896 – 1930

No. 2 burner, 1" wick; 1 quart font.
Cold blast globe, plain or with bull's-eye lens.
Cold blast.
Finish: bright tin or japanned blue.

Common.

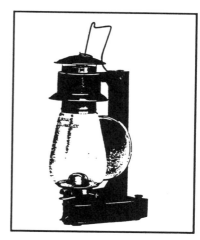

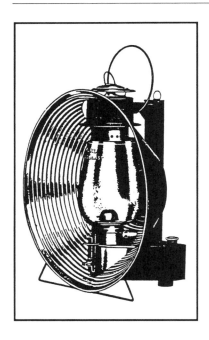

Headlight
1905 – 1930

No. 2 burner, 1" wick; 1 3/4 quart font.
7" diameter, nickel-plated reflector; 16"
concentric corrugated hood.
Cold blast.
Finish: bright tin, enameled brown.

One of the most common of Buhl's
lanterns and a "best seller;" used
on farms in milk houses and barns.

Common.

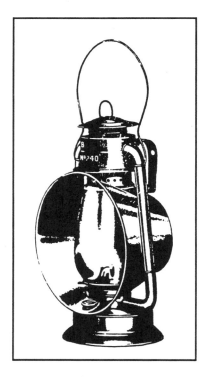

Inspector
1913 – 1930

No. 2 burner, 1" wick; 1 1/2 pint font.
Globe plain or with bull's-eye lens;
6" diameter, nickel-plated brass reflector
with large hood.
Cold blast.
Finish: tin or japanned blue.

Prior to 1913 this model was called the
240 series. Its different numbers (e.g.,
240, 241) were given for color and
other variations in options.

Perfect when a powerful concentrated
light was required.

Rare.

Vehicle Lantern
1913 – 1930

Height: 12".
No. 0 burner, 5/8" wick.
No. 00 globe, plain or with bull's-eye lens;
red lens set in polished corrugated reflector.
Cold blast.
Finish: re-tinned and enameled black.

Threw a bright light to the front. Had a
2" red warning light to the rear.

Furnished with dash mount attachments.

Prior to 1913 this was called the
No. 25 lantern.

This lantern met the requirements
of new vehicular laws that were being
enacted in many states. It also made a
useful hand lantern.

Common.

Conquest
1913 – 1930

No. 1 burner, 5/8" wick.
No. 0 globe, in clear or red.
Hot blast.
Finish: bright tin.

From 1888-1913 this was called the
No. 17. Unlike the Conquest it did not
have a domed font.

Common.

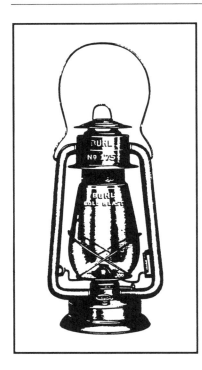

Hurricane
1888 – 1930

No. 00: 1888 – 1915
No. 0 brass burner, 5/8" wick;
1 pint, flat-top font.
Finish: tin or brass.

No. 1: 1913 – 1930
No. 1 steel burner, 5/8" wick;
1 1/8 pint, domed-top font.
Finish: tin or japanned blue.

No. 2: 1913 – 1930
No. 2 burner, 1" wick; 1 1/2 pint,
domed-top font.
Cold blast.
Finish: bright tin, japanned blue, all brass;
font, re-tinned copper or all brass.

All models: clear, red, blue and green globes available.

This series of lanterns was available enameled to buyer's choice of color.

Common: all models.

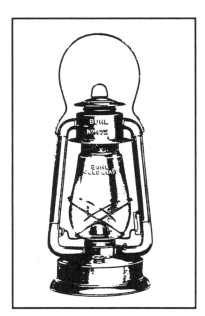

Majestic
1913 – 1930

No. 2 burner, 1" wick; 2 3/4 pint font.
Cold blast.
Finish: bright tin, or bright tin with copper
font buffed to bright shine, then lacquered.

Pre-1913, font top was flat; after 1913, font top was domed.

Manufactured with many different model numbers, but design remained the same.

Common.

Little Giant
1913 – 1930

Height: 13".
No. 2 burner, 1" wick; 1 1/2 pint font.
Cold blast.
Finish: bright tin; bright tin with brass font;
bright tin with brass font having brass
canopy; bright tin with copper font.
Short globe, in clear blue, red, amber
or green.
Fonts could be left buff, or lacquered
or re-tinned.

Pre-1913, manufactured with many
different model numbers, but design
remained the same.

Common.

Eclipse
1913 – 1930

No. 1 burner; 5/8" wick; 1 3/8 pint font.
No. 0 globe, bull's-eye or plain;
concentric corrugated reflector.
Hot blast.
Finish: bright tin or japanned blue.

Rare.

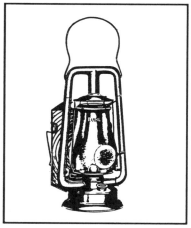

Hurricane No. 2 Reflector
1910 – 1930

No. 2 burner; 1" wick; 1 1/2 pint font.
Cold blast globe, bull's-eye or plain;
concentric corrugated reflector.
Cold blast.
Finish: bright tin or japanned blue.

Pre-1913, font tops were flat; post-1913
font tops were dome-shaped.

Rare.

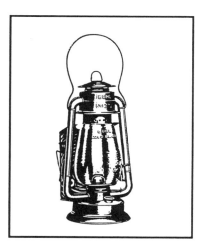

C.T. Ham Manufacturing Company

Charles Trafton Ham was born in Maine in September, 1824. By his twenties Ham was a locomotive engineer with the Boston and Lowell Railroad. In 1871 he became a partner in the J. H. Kelly Company, a lantern manufacturer, where he spent five years before selling his interest back to Kelly.

During this time Ham apparently learned the lantern-manufacturing process, which served him well when he then became a partner in the Buffalo Steam Gauge Company of Buffalo, New York. This company manufactured and sold headlights and other lighting-related items. During 1878, with its name changed to the Buffalo Steam Gauge and Lantern Company, it moved to Rochester, New York. C. T. Ham served as its president until 1881, when the company was purchased by the Jenny syndicate. At this point Ham left the company, which continued under new ownership as the Steam Gauge and Lantern Company.

In 1886 Ham opened the C. T. Ham Manufacturing Company and by 1890 had a very large factory at 731 Oak Street in Rochester, with as many as 260 employees. At the Lantern Association's annual meeting on January 13, 1892, Ham gave his lantern-production figures for the prior year as 29,043 dozen.

Charles T. Ham died on September 27, 1903, and the company was continued by his son, George William Ham, who died in 1915. Shortly afterwards the company's manufacturing equipment and customer accounts were sold to the R. E. Dietz Company and C.T. Ham Company was closed. The Rochester city directory lists the C.T.Ham Company buildings as vacant in 1915. Any C. T. Ham lanterns you may find are therefore pre-1915.

All Ham products are marked "C. T. Ham" on the top or font. Lanterns that have rounded font tops, with a few exceptions, can be dated as being manufactured after 1902. This type of font became popular because of its ability to readily shed rain water, and for its hot- and cold-blast designs in which an air chamber was created above the fuel, adding strength to the lantern.

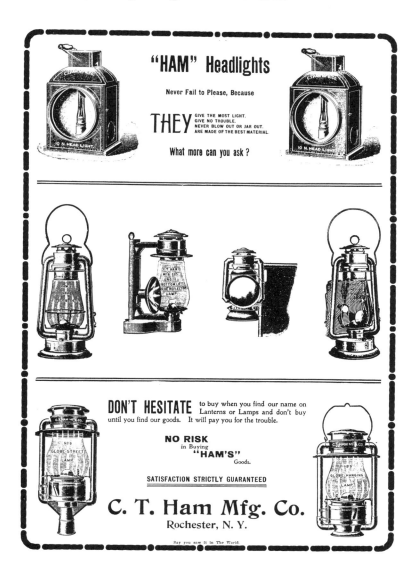

A late 19th-century advertisement for Ham Lanterns.

C.T. Ham Manufacturing Co., circa 1913.

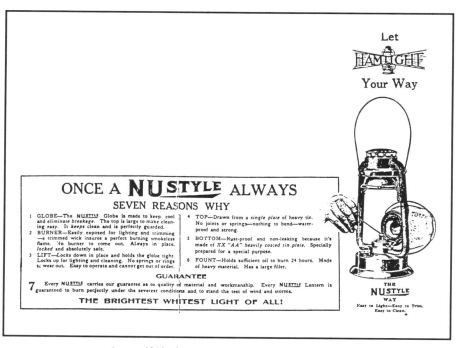

A circa 1913 advertisement for the Nu-Style Lantern.

No. 2 Side Spring Safety Lantern
1887 – 1914

No. 2 burner, 1" "B" wick, large oil font.
Hot blast.
No. 0 globe, clear, ruby, green, or blue.
Finish: tin; tin, copper plated; tin, brass
plated; all brass; brass, nickel plated.

The side springs, when lowered, securely held the globe on the glass flanges.

Rare.

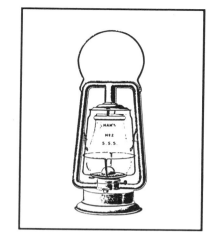

No. 0 Clipper Lift Lantern
1887 – 1914

No. 1 locked burner, 5/8" "A" wick.
No. 0 globe.
Hot blast.
Finish: tin; tin, copper plated; tin, brass
plated; all brass; brass, nickel plated.

A very serviceable lantern strongly made. The font re-tinned to prevent leakage. Also called the **Clipper**.

Common.

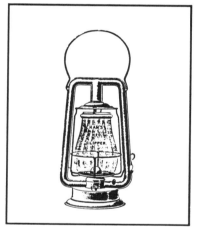

No. 1 Clipper Lift Lantern
1900 – 1914

No. 1 burner, 5/8" "A" wick.
No. 0 globe, clear, ruby, green, or blue.
Cold blast.
Finish: tin.

The light obtained from this lantern was far brighter than that from the No. 0 Clipper Lift hot-blast lantern. Price in 1910 was $1.12; 25 cents extra for colored globe.

Common.

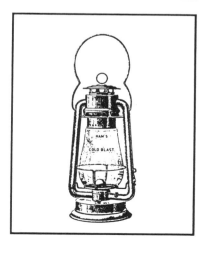

No. 2 Clipper Lift Lantern
1887 – 1914

No. 2 locked burner, 1" "B" wick.
No. 0 globe, clear, ruby, green or blue.
Hot blast.
Finish: tin; tin, copper plated; tin, brass plated; all brass; brass, nickel plated.
Font re-tinned to prevent leakage; globe easily removed for cleaning.

Price for tin was $1.09; brass, nickel-plated version cost $3.84.

Common.

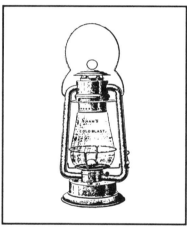

No. 2 Two Piece
Tube Lantern
1898 – 1914

No. 2 burner, 1" "B" wick.
No. 0 globe.
Cold blast.
Finish: tin; all brass; brass, nickel plated.

Very good construction for use in strong drafts. Used in lumber camps and places where there was dust, as burner did not clog.

Common.

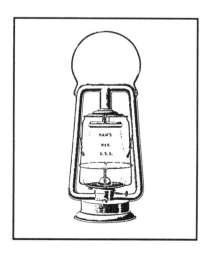

No. 0 Side Spring
Safety Lantern
1898 – 1914

No. 1 burner, 5/8", "A" wick.
No. 0 globe.
Hot blast.
Finish: tin; tin, copper plated; tin, brass plated; all brass; brass, nickel plated.

Globe was easily raised and lowered because the side springs rested on its smooth glass surface.

Common.

No. 0 Glass Fount Clipper Lift Lantern
1900 – 1914

No. 1 burner, 5/8" "A" wick.
No. 0 globe, clear, ruby, green, or blue.
Hot blast.
Finish: tin.

Had a removable glass font, securely fastened when installed. Extra glass fonts cost 10 cents each.

Very rare.

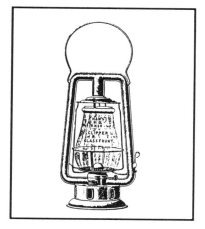

No. 0 Glass Fount Side Spring Safety Lantern
1900 – 1914

No. 1 burner, 5/8" "A" wick.
No. 0 globe.
Hot blast.
Finish: tin.

Had locked burner and removable glass font. Main purchasers of this lantern were construction companies.

Very rare.

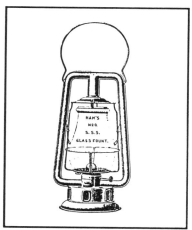

No. 0 Handy Lantern
1897 – 1914

No. 1 burner, 5/8" "A" wick.
No. 0 globe, clear, ruby, green, or blue.
Hot blast.
Finish: tin.

Had a sliding door in the base plate to make it easy to light the wick.

Rare.

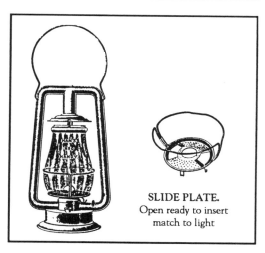

SLIDE PLATE.
Open ready to insert
match to light

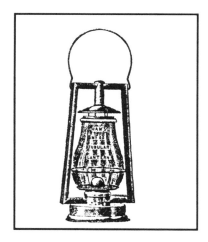

No. 00 Jewel Oval Tube Lantern
1887 – 1914

No. 0 burner, 1/2" No. 0 wick.
Gem globe.
Finish: tin; tin, copper plated; tin, brass plated.

Smaller than the No. 1 and No. 0 sizes; the lantern gave a nice light. Priced at 75 cents for tin and $1.08 for copper-plate.

Rare.

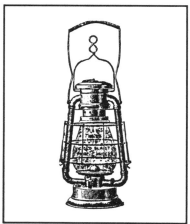

Gem Tin Tubular Lantern
1900 – 1914

Gem cold blast burner, 5/8" "A" wick.
Gem globe, clear or colors.
Cold blast.
Finish: tin.

Well-made, small lantern; useful around the home and carriage house.

Common.

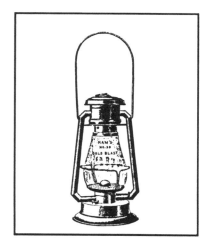

No. 39 Round Tube Lantern
1887 – 1914

Gem cold blast burner, 5/8" "A" wick.
No. 39 cold blast plain or bull's-eye globe.
Cold blast.
Finish: brass; brass, nickel plated.

Strongly built; a very popular lantern. In 1902, sold for $4.17 each.

Rare.

No. 39 Tin Mill Lantern
1887 – 1914

Gem cold blast burner, 5/8" "A" wick.
No. 39 globe.
Cold blast.
Finish: tin, nickel plated.
Available with or without lock attachment.

This lantern was constructed of heavy gauge tin, designed to keep the dust out of its side tubes and "every precaution has been taken to make it safe for use in flour mills, and saw mills." Its safety was endorsed by many insurance companies.

Very rare.

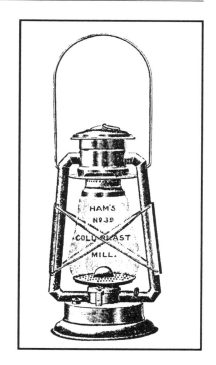

No. 2 Tin Mill Lantern
1887 – 1914

No. 2 burner, 1" "B" wick.
No. 0 globe.
Hot blast.
Finish: tin.
Available with or without lock.
Shown with lock attached.

For use by watchmen in mills. Could not be opened during use, which reduced fire risk.

Very rare.

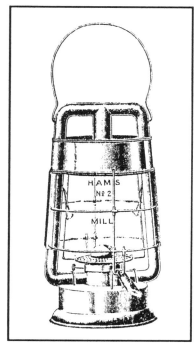

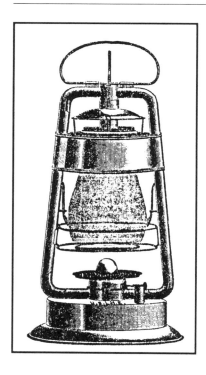

No. 1 U.S.L.E. (Lighthouse Engineer's) Tin Lantern
1887 – 1914

No. 1 burner, 5/8" "B" wick.
No. 1 clear globe.
Hot blast.
Finish: tin.
Shown with globe raised. Ruby, green, or blue globe added to this lantern cost an extra $1.00.

Used by the government for placing on buoys. Notice the raised filler tube to prevent oil slurping out of the fill hole. Was available with lock, for insurance purposes, to prevent careless refilling where light was required for long periods.

Very rare.

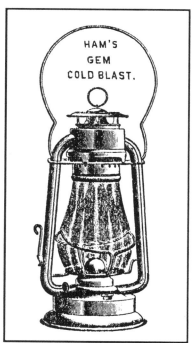

Gem Brass Lantern
1887 – 1914

No. 1 burner, 5/8" "A" wick.
Gem globe.
Cold blast.
Finish: all brass; brass, nickel plated.
Clipper lift attachment.

Polished finish and convenient size made this an attractive portable lantern. It was claimed to give more light than any other lantern with a 5/8" wick.

Common.

No. 2 "E Z E" Lantern
1887 – 1914

No. 2 burner, 1" wick.
Hot blast.
Finish: tin.

Utilitarian model for people who needed a low-cost lantern.

Common.

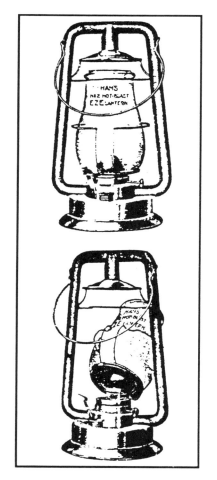

Shown with globe tilted for cleaning.

No. 39 Brass Round Tube Lantern
1897 – 1902

Gem burner, 5/8" "A" wick.
No. 39 cold blast globe.
Cold blast.
Finish: all brass; brass, nickel plated.

A high grade lantern, finely finished. Very high price ($4.17) for a lantern, which may have reduced its sales.

Common.

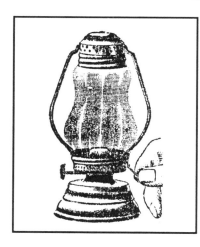

Cadet Brass Lantern
1887 – 1914

Dead flame.
Finish: all brass.

Suitable for skating and household use. This was a popular lantern.

Common.

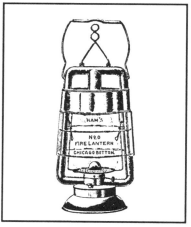

No. 0 Brass Fireman's Lantern
1887 – 1914

No. 1 burner, 5/8" wick.
No. 0 globe.
Hot blast.
Finish: all brass; brass, nickel plated.

Designed for use in burning buildings. The lantern was shielded to keep hose water from entering the globe.

Very rare.

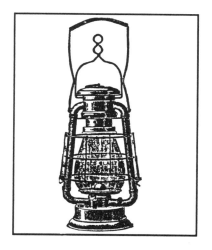

No. 39 Brass Chief Lantern
1887 – 1914

Gem burner, 5/8" "A" wick.
No. 39 cold blast globe.
Cold blast.
Finish: all brass; brass, nickel plated.

A fine quality lantern, with a wire-wound bail handle for added grip and extra strong guards to protect globe.

Very rare.

No. 2 Brass Fire Lantern
1887 – 1914

No. 2 cold blast burner, 1" "B" wick.
No. 0 cold blast globe.
Cold blast.
Finish: all brass; brass, nickel plated.

Gave much brighter light than the No. 39 Fireman's Hooded Lantern. "Maintains light in smoky buildings." Also called the **President.**

Very rare.

No. 0 Brass Side Spring Fireman's Lantern
1887 – 1914

No. 1 burner, 5/8" "A" wick.
No. 0 globe.
Hot blast.
Finish: all brass; brass, nickel plated.

Intended for use where a medium weight lantern was required. In fire company trials and tests with other manufacturers' fire lantern products, this lantern was often chosen over others.
Also known as the **Captain.**

Very rare.

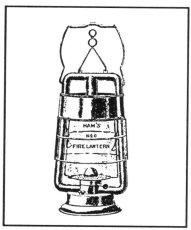

No. 39 Fireman's Hooded Lantern
1887 – 1914

5/8", lard oil ratchet burner.
No. 39 globe.
Dead flame.

Finish: all brass; brass, nickel plated.

For fire department use. Flame could be adjusted by outside ratchet.

Very rare.

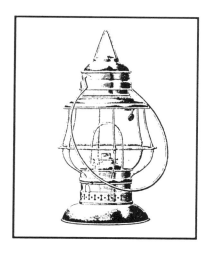

No. 39 Ring Top Brass Fireman's Lantern
1887 – 1914

5/8", lard oil ratchet burner.
No. 39 globe.
Dead flame.
Finish: all brass; brass, nickel plated.

For fire department use. Strongly made lantern, intended for use where a lower-priced lantern was required.

Very rare.

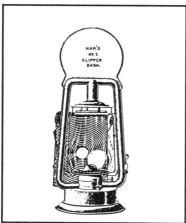

No. 2 Clipper Lift Tin Dash Lantern
1897 – 1914

No. 2 burner, 1" "B" wick, large font.
No. 0 plain or bull's-eye globe.
Hot blast.
Finish: tin or japanned blue.

The tin reflector was corrugated to help the bull's-eye lens focus the light.

Common

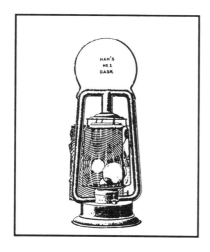

No. 2 Side Spring Tin Dash Lantern
1897 – 1914

No. 2 locked burner, 1" "B" wick.
No. 0 plain or bull's-eye globe.
Hot blast.
Finish: tin or japanned blue.

The font was re-tinned to prevent leakage. Also available with clipper lift.

Common.

No. 15 Clipper Lift
Tin Dash Lantern
1897 – 1914

No. 1 burner, 5/8", "A" wick.
Plain or bull's-eye globe.
Hot blast.
Finish: tin or japanned blue.

The most popular dash lantern sold by
this company.

Very common.

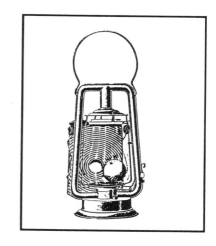

No. 15 Side Spring
Tin Dash Lantern
1897 – 1914

No. 1 locked burner, 5/8" "A" wick.
No. 0 plain or bull's-eye globe.
Hot blast.
Finish: tin or japanned blue.

Common.

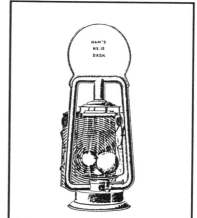

No. 0 Hood Reflector
Tin Dash Lantern
1887 – 1902

No. 1 high-cone burner, 5/8" "A" wick.
No. 0 globe, plain or bull's-eye;
5" silvered-glass reflector.
Hot blast.
Finish: tin or japanned blue.

Also available with a rear handle,
as used on the No. 2 Railroad Inspector's
Lantern. Also called the **Senator.**
1902-1914: called **Empire Car Inspector's
Lantern;** handle added and bail attached
to side tubes instead of top.

Rare.

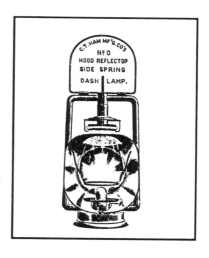

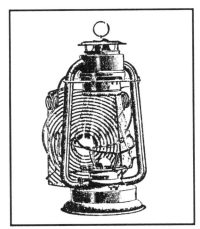

Gem Tin Dash Lantern
1902 – 1914

Gem cold blast burner, 5/8" "A" wick.
Gem globe.
Cold blast.
Finish: tin or japanned.

For use where a small dash lantern was
needed. Also called the **Clipper Tin
Dash.**

Common.

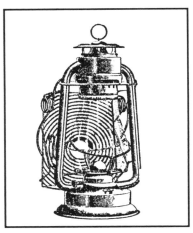

Gem Brass Dash Lantern
1898 – 1914

Gem cold blast burner, 5/8" "A" wick.
Gem globe.
Cold blast.
Finish: all brass; brass, nickel plated.

The dash attachment for this lantern was
removable; finished in tin or bronzed or
nickel plated. Very desirable for doctor's
use or anyone requiring a small, neat
lantern. Common.

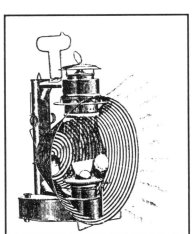

No. 20 Tin Searchlight
1900 – 1914

No. 2 cold blast burner, 1" "B" wick.
No. 0 cold blast plain or bull's-eye globe.
Cold blast.
Finish: japanned blue or tin.

This lantern was continued (with small
design changes) into the Dietz sales line
after Ham was bought by Dietz. It threw
a brilliant and steady light, ideal for use
in stables, barns, mills, packing houses,
summer resorts, etc.
Also called the **X.I.L. Searchlight.**

Common.

No. 11 Cold Blast
Tin Lantern
1900 – 1914

No. 1 burner, 5/8" "A" wick.
No. 0 globe; 5" silvered reflector.
Cold blast.
Finish: tin; tin, japanned blue; tin, brass
plated; tin, copper plated.

Used a patent wind break, similar to that
used on street lamps. Would not blow
out in strong wind.

Rare.

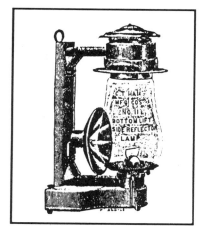

No. 12 Cold Blast
Tin Lantern
1900 – 1914

No. 2 burner, 1" "B" wick.
No. 0 cold blast globe; 6" silvered reflector.
Cold blast.
Finish: tin; tin, japanned blue; tin, brass
plated; tin, copper plated.

Could be hung on a wall or carried
by hand. Also called the **Genesee.**

Rare.

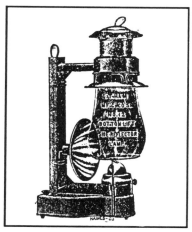

No. 18 Cold Blast
Driving Lantern
1890 – 1914

Height: 10".
1/2" kerosene burner.
4" double convex lens; 4" silvered reflector.
Cold blast.
Finish: tin; tin, black enameled or
nickel plated.

Lighted the road for 100 feet
ahead of a carriage. Two styles
of brackets available.

Rare.

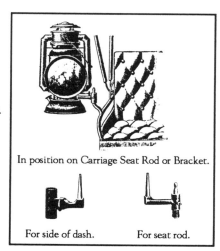

In position on Carriage Seat Rod or Bracket.

For side of dash.   For seat rod.

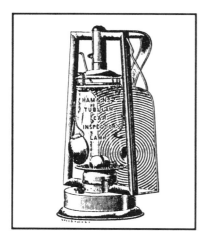

No. 2 Railroad Inspector's Lantern
1887 – 1914

No. 2 kerosene burner, 1" "B" wick.
No. 0 bull's-eye or plain globe.
Hot blast.

Specially adapted for inspecting cars and for the engineer's use. The reflector, in combination with the bull's-eye lens, gave a focused beam of light.

Rare.

Bull's-Eye or Dark Police Lantern
1887 – 1914

Height of lens: 2 3/4".
Finish: tin or black enamel.
Dead flame.

Made for police and fire companies, but also available for general sales.

Common.

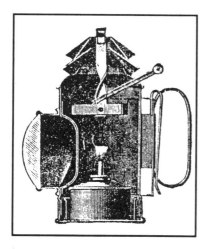

Bull's-Eye or Dark Police Lantern
1887 – 1914

Height of lens: 3".
Finish: tin or black enamel.
Dead flame
With flash attachment.

Identical lantern available from R.E. Dietz Company.

Rare.

No. 9 Globe
Hanging Lantern
1887 – 1914

No. 9 burner, 1 1/2" "D" wick.
Fonts available in tin, glass, brass,
or copper.
No. 9 globe.
Cold blast.
Finish: tin, painted your color.

1887 – 1900: side tubes were soldered
into corner pieces.

Shown: 1900 – 1914.

With a post attachment, sold as the
Street Lantern.

Had an automatic light extinguisher so
the lamplighter could set the lantern to
go out after a predetermined number of
hours: 4, 8, 12, 16, 20 or 24.

Rare: both models.

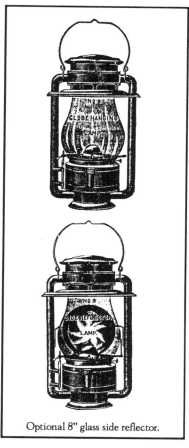

Optional 8" glass side reflector.

No. 10 Square Tubular Street
Lamp
1890 – 1914

No. 10 burner, 1 1/2" "D" wick.
Cold blast.
Finish: painted green, or color
of your choice.

Outside wick adjuster. Automatic timer
to extinguish light at predetermined
times. "Will not blow out in the
strongest of winds. Flame will not strike
near the glass, which in the past has
caused excessive glass breakage in other
manufacturers products."

Very rare.

No. 17 Tin Dash Lantern
1890 – 1914

No. 2 cold blast burner, 1" "B" wick.
No. 0 plain or bull's-eye globe.
Cold blast.
Finish: tin or japanned blue.

This lantern was intended for use where a more powerful light was required than that from the No. 15 Dash Lantern. Also called the **Sterling.**

Rare.

Nu-Style Lantern
1912 – 1914

No. 2 burner, 1" wick.
Hot blast.
Finish: tin; tin, copper plated; tin, brass plated; all brass; tin with copper font; and tin with brass top and font.

This lantern was designed by Warren McArthur, who was the sole sales agent for C.T. Ham Company (as well as for Dietz, in 1912).

After Dietz purchased C.T. Ham Company, this lantern was sold by R.E. Dietz as the "D-Lite." It became one of the best selling lanterns in the Dietz line.

Rare.

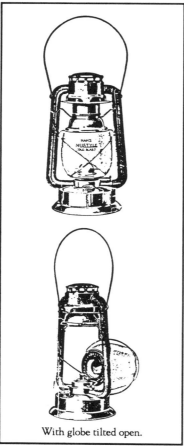

With globe tilted open.

No. 5 Triangular Lantern
1887 – 1910

No. "D" burner, 1 1/2" wick.
10" silvered, round reflector.
Cold blast.
Finish: tin, painted black.

Used for railroad stations, bridges, stables, mills, packing houses, large halls, etc.

Very rare.

No. 6 Square Lantern
1887 – 1914

Cold blast.
Finish: tin, painted black.

Shown is the later (1900 – 1914) improved version of the No. 6. The earlier (1887 – 1900) style can be recognized by a square, corrugated rear reflector.

Very rare.

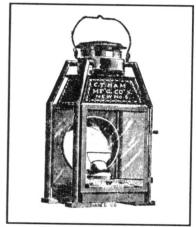

No. 7 and No. 8 Square Bridge Lanterns
1887 – 1910

Cold blast burner, 1 1/2" "D" wick.
Silvered, corrugated rear reflector.
Finish: tin, painted black.
No. 8 was larger than No. 7.

For use on bridges, locks and waterways.

Very rare.

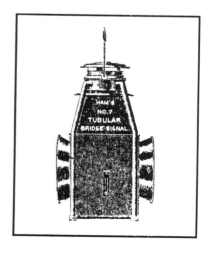

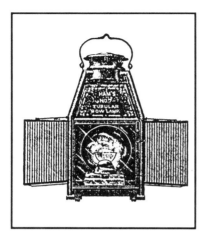

Bow Lamp
1887 – 1914

No. 7 cold blast burner.
Silvered, corrugated rear reflector,
with swing-out side reflectors.
Finish: tin, painted black.

Used on boats as a front light. Also available with a socket mount for mounting on a pole. Very rare.

No. 7 Square
Government Lamp
1887 – 1906

No. 2 burner, 1" "D" wick.
1887 – 1900: square. Silvered reflector.
Dead flame (shown).

1900 – 1906: round. 8" silvered reflector.
Hot blast.
Finish: tin, painted black.
Available with or without guards.

Designed exclusively for the government but available to the general public.

Very rare.

No. 8 Square Lantern
1900 – 1914

Height: 24 1/2"; width: 13 1/2";
depth: 11 1/2"; weight: 11 lbs.
No. 8 cold blast burner, 1 1/2" "D" wick.
10" round, silvered reflector.
Cold blast.
Finish: tin, painted black.
Furnished with or without guards.
Shown is improved version. The early version can be recognized by its square, (not round) corrugated reflector. Advertised as having light output equal to any gas jet light. Designed to be used in packing houses and saw mills. Very rare.

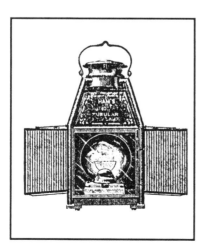

Pole Target or
Mast Head Lantern
1887 – 1914

Globe: clear, green, or ruby glass.
Also available in those colors as a
Fresnel lens (shown).
Dead flame.
Finish: tin.

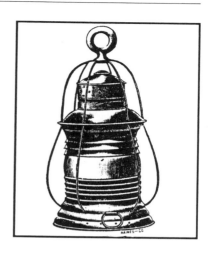

For boat or ship use. Main market would
have been barges on canals and rivers.
Prior to 1906, manufactured by H.A.J.
Helvig; then manufactured by Bristol
Brass Company and sold by National
Marine Lamp Company until 1913; from
1913 to 1914, manufactured by National
Marine Lamp Company.

Rare.

Moehring Burner
Manufactured by Plume and Atwood
Manufacturing Company, the Moehring
burner was recognized as the standard
for railroad use. As in the headlight
shown here, it was used in trolley and
tram lights as well as railroad train lights.
It required the use of a chimney.

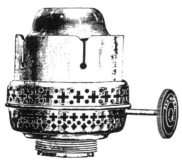

Moehring Burner

Diamond Lantern
1900 – 1914

Cold blast.
Finish: tin, painted black.

This driving lantern was made to be used with the new automobiles. With wick trimmed and adjusted, its light shone over 150 feet.

Rare.

Argus Lantern
1900 – 1914

Finish: tin, painted black.

Used where a smaller lantern than the Diamond was required. Its bevelled lens was advertised as focusing the light for better highway visibility at greater speeds.

Rare.

Conductor's Lantern
1887 – 1914

Sperm oil burner.
Globe handmade of best flint glass; clear,
ruby, green, blue, half-green, half-ruby,
and half-blue.
Finish: highly polished brass;
nickel-, silver-, and gold-plated brass.
8 styles were offered, having subtle design
differences in bail, tops, guards, etc.
Engraving on the globe cost: Name: $1.00.
Name with wreath: $1.50.

Also available were handsome, plush-lined morocco leather cases specially made for the lanterns.

Very rare.

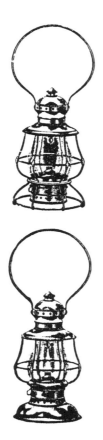

New Style.
Hinged Top.

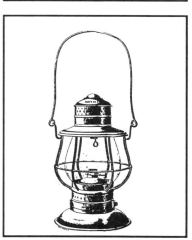

Old Style.
Hinged Bottom.

Lake and River Tin Lanterns
1887 – 1914

Sperm oil or kerosene burner.
Finish: tin.

Old style manufactured by Steam Gauge and Lantern Company between 1887 and 1897, and appeared in both the Dietz and Ham catalogues. New style was manufactured by Ham. Used mainly on river and lake steamers.

Very rare.

No. 39 Railroad Lantern
1887 – 1914

Double or single globe guards available.
Dead flame.
Finish: tin.

Spring bail, double steel-wire supports.

This lantern went through several style changes, including: wire base after 1910 and outside wick raiser after 1912.

Common.

Standard Railroad Lantern
1897 – 1902

Sperm oil or kerosene burner.
Finish: tin.

Available with single- or double-wire guard and tin or wire base. Bail could stand upright or lie down as required.

Rare.

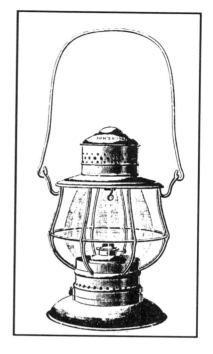

Oval Top Railroad Tail Lamp
1887 – 1900

Finish: tin, painted black.

Available with single- or double-semaphore lens or bull's-eye lens.

Very rare.

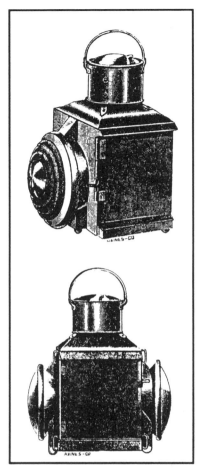

Railroad Tail Lamp
1900 – 1914

Finish: heavy gauge tin, painted black.

Available with single- or double-semaphore lens or bull's-eye lens.

Very rare

No. 1, 2 and 3 Square Station Lamps
1887 – 1902

Furnished in three sizes.

No. 1. Small.
*Height: 12"; width: 8"; weight: 4 lbs.
5/8" wick; 7" reflector.*

No. 2. Medium.
*Height: 14"; width: 10"; weight: 6 lbs.
1" wick; 8", reflector.*

No. 3. Large.
*Height: 16"; width: 12"; weight: 8 lbs.
1" wick; 10" reflector.*

*Cold blast, all models.
All with burner, chimney and reflector.
Finish: painted black.*

Available in packed cases: one each, or three together as shown here.

Rare.

Marker or Rear Signal Lamp
1887 – 1914

Corrugated, 4" lens in any color ordered.
Cold blast.
Finish: heavy gauge tin, painted black.

This lamp was designed to be used on the rear of passenger trains, one on each corner of the car.

Very rare.

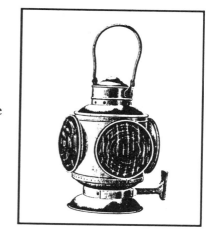

Marker or Rear Signal Lamp
1900 – 1914

Cold blast.
Finish: heavy gauge tin, painted black.

Also sold as the **Blizzard** with different mounting bracket, and used as an engine signal lamp. For use on passenger trains.

Very rare.

Ten Inch Traction
Engine Headlight
1887 – 1914

Height: 21 3/4"; width: 12"; depth: 9 1/2".
Moehring burner with circular wick, 5" long.
Chimney: No. 87 Ham's.
10" reflector made of copper, which was then nickel plated and finished with silver plating.
Finish: painted black.
Dead flame.

"The light will not jar out on rough roads."

Very rare.

Ten Inch Motor Headlight
1887 – 1914

Moehring burner with 5" long circular wick.
Chimney: No. 87 Ham's.
Finish: painted black.
Dead flame.

Same size and specifications as Traction Headlight, but with dash mounting bracket, so it could be used on cable and electric cars as well as railroad switch engines.

Very rare.

Cab Lamps
1887 – 1914

Finish: all brass or bright nickel.
Dead flame.

Called "gauge lamps" by some other lantern companies. Used to light instruments in the engine compartment.

Very rare.

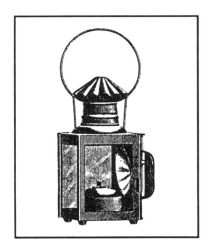

Square Railroad Signal Lamp
1887 – 1908

Silvered reflector.
Finish: tin, painted black.
Dead flame.

For railroad car inspectors. This lantern was offered in the Dietz catalog 1906 through 1908.

Rare.

Railroad Inspector's Lamp
1887 – 1914

4" glass reflector; 5" glass front.
Finish: tin, painted black.
Dead flame.
Showed a red, green, or clear light
as desired.
Also available with clear glass only.

This lantern was offered in the Dietz catalogue, 1906 – 1908. Also called the **Tricolor Inspector's Lantern.**

Rare.

Switch Target Railroad Lamp
1887 – 1902

4" or 5 3/8" semaphore lens.
Finish: heavy gauge tin, painted black.
Dead flame.

Shown with sliding door open to access the burner.

Very rare.

Switch Target Railroad Lamp
1900 – 1914

4" or 5 3/8" semaphore lens, in any color or color combination desired.
Finish: heavy gauge tin, painted black.
Dead flame.

Shown with sliding door open to access the burner.

Very rare.

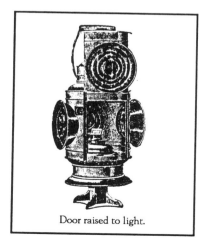

Door raised to light.

Angle Lamp Company

During the late 19th and early 20th centuries there was great competition among manufacturers to produce new forms of lighting. In cities, illuminating gas had begun to be available to homes, but rural areas still had to rely on kerosene as a lighting source. Out of the endless variety of lamps and lanterns available appeared the "Angle," which was a new concept and became quite popular. Its only manufacturer in the United States was the Angle Lamp Company, at 76 Park Place, New York City. Angle Lamp operated from 1890 to 1920 and employed up to 300 people at the height of production. The years 1895 to 1910 saw Angle's greatest sales.

The operating system of the Angle lamp differed from all previous kerosene lamps, as the burner and wick extended from the side of the lantern at an almost right angle. This doubled the light available, as the brightest part of the flame was the flat side of the wick facing down. The light was therefore thrown downward rather than in all directions. This was a great feature for reading or any situation where light was needed in a downward direction. These lamps were very ornate, with colored globes and attractive brass or copper fonts, and designed to be used in the home. A more utilitarian version of these lamps was advertised by many distributors as being ideal for pool tables and bowling alleys.

The company offered only one outside portable lantern, which was actually an Angle lamp mounted inside a glass case to protect its flame from the weather. It was claimed to have light output of forty candlepower, which was quite bright compared to the average six candlepower obtained from the kerosene outdoor lanterns available at that time.

Angle Lantern

Oil capacity: 1 quart.
Burned 12 hours.
Finish: plain tin, double plated;
frame: iron, painted black.

This was called the "Ideal" and was sold overseas extensively.

Had a glass bottom so light could be thrown downward.

Side view of lantern assembly.

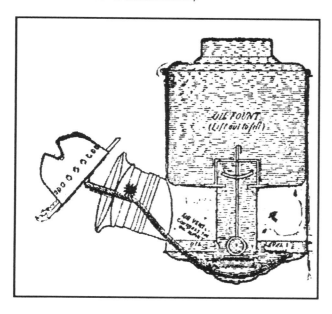

This drawing shows how the oil was constantly fed at an even rate to the wick in the Angle lamp. The font supplied oil to the reservoir by way of a float valve that maintained oil level in the wick well. This ensured that the wick was saturated in oil at all times, thus maintaining a constant, even flame. To light the wick, the globe holder was raised and a match applied. To extinguish the light, the flame was turned down quickly to cut off the fuel. The oil font could be removed and refilled without extinguishing the flame.

Hurwood Manufacturing Company;
John A. Hurley, Inc.

This company, which fabricated screw drivers, awls, chucks and lanterns, was started in 1903 with John A. Hurley as president. In 1909 the company changed its name to John A. Hurley, Inc. It continued to operate under this name until 1915, at 1565 Railroad Avenue, Bridgeport, Connecticut. After 1915 the company closed, and its manufacturing buildings were occupied by other unrelated businesses. Coincidentally with the closing, an insurance brokerage opened that same year in Bridgeport under the name of John A. Hurley, but there is no evidence this is the same person.

Many of this company's lanterns were marked "Aladdin" but they may have made other models as well. Research indicates there is no connection between Hurwood/Hurley, Inc. and the Mantle Lamp Company, which manufactured the more well-known Aladdin glass table lamps and portable pressurized-fuel gasoline lanterns.

Hurley lanterns have a very distinctive style of globe lifter and globe holder, easily distinguishable by the globe being held in place by a wire loop fastened to a single sliding arm. This system patent was filed on November 18, 1907, by Knut Ludwig Stendahl, who was an employee of Hurwood Manufacturing Company in 1906.

Lanterns marked "Hurley Inc." were manufactured after 1909. Lanterns marked "Aladdin" are also marked on the font "Pat Sept 8 08" and "John A. Hurley, Inc." These lanterns also were manufactured after 1909.

Aladdin-Marked Lanterns
1909 – 1915

Finish: bright tin or painted black.

Recognizable by the distinctive globe holder and globe raising system; unlike any other manufacturer's.

Very rare.

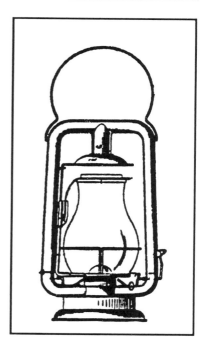

Keystone Lantern Company

The Keystone Lantern Company was established in 1903 and located at the corner of Chestnut and Broad Streets, in Philadelphia. During 1905 the company moved to a new location at Portico Street, in Germantown. Around 1912 it moved again, to the corner of Tacony and Cottman Streets in Philadelphia. These addresses are for the most part office buildings, indicating that Keystone may have been a lantern distributor rather than a manufacturer. After 1930 it is no longer listed in the city directories.

One of their most popular lanterns was the "Casey," presumably named after John T. Casey, who in 1902 patented his invention of the wick-raiser system found on many Casey lanterns. Casey was an officer of Keystone, serving in various capacities until about 1920. After that date he is no longer listed in the company directory.

Lanterns marked "Casey" were manufactured from 1916 to 1921 by Perkins Marine Lamp Corporation, and sold by Keystone. It is not known if they were manufactured by any company prior to 1916. An "extra-galvanized" marine version of the Casey lantern was available as late as 1924 from Perkins. Nearly all lanterns with Casey wick raisers that the author has seen have been railroad-marked or railroad-style dead-flame lanterns. None of the railroad-marked Caseys were for marine use. Household lanterns sold by this company do not have the Casey wick raiser, but are usually marked with a drawing of a key and often, but not always, are marked "Keystone " or "Keystoneware."

Casey Lantern
1916 – 1921

Height: 11"; base diameter 7 1/4".
Burner: kerosene or signal oil.
Globe: 3 1/2" diameter, 5 1/8" high;
available in choice of colors.
Dead flame.
Finish: tinned steel for land;
extra-galvanized for marine use.

Manufactured for Keystone by Perkins Marine Lamp Corporation, this was a popular lantern with railroad companies but it was also sold as a deck or signal lantern for marine use. A limited quantity were manufactured with a closed base. A wax (vaclite) font and burner was available for 50 cents extra.

The statement "its all in the turn" refers to the unique wick raiser used on this lantern. Unlike standard wick raisers, this one could be operated with ease even in cold weather with the user wearing gloves.

Common: with open frame base.

Common: with railroad markings.

Rare: with closed base.

Rare: with no railroad markings.

Very rare: with ship markings.

Very rare: with Vaclite font.

Rayo Lanterns

The trademark "Rayo" was registered to Standard Oil Company, Bayonne, New Jersey (filed on September 4, 1906, and placed into use October 2, 1906), for a table lamp with a special burner and a round wick. These table lamps, marked "Rayo" and dated "1905" on the burner top, were initially manufactured by Edward Miller and Sons Company of Connecticut.

Rayo lamps and later, Rayo lanterns, were distributed by a subdivision of Standard Oil Company referred to as the "burning products division," which became formally known as Socony Petroleum Products Division. The purpose of this oil-burning products group was to sell products, such as lanterns, that used oil and kerosene. They were to be sold cheaply on the assumption that they would become popular and thus would stimulate sales of the main products the company manufactured: illuminating oil and kerosene.

By 1907, lamps marked "Rayo" were still primarily manufactured by Edward Miller, but were also being manufactured by other companies, such as the Scovill Manufacturing Company, the Manhattan Brass Company, and the Cleveland Foundry Company. Other lamps manufactured expressly for Socony by these companies can be found marked "Sterling" and "Perfection."

Beginning that same year, lanterns of various designs, but all marked "Rayo," were manufactured for Standard Oil by Defiance Lantern and Stamping Company, Perkins Marine Lamp Corporation, R. E. Dietz Company, Embury Manufacturing Company, Pritchard-Strong Company, and many others. By the end of 1907, Standard Oil's total sales of Rayo-marked burning devices came to 485,000, including lamps and lanterns, stoves and heaters.

By 1908 Rayo lamps and lanterns were in such demand that the manufacturers contracted to supply the lamps and lanterns could not keep up with orders. At the Standard Oil Company's annual meeting in 1908 it was noted that sales of Rayo lamps, lanterns and other products could have been five times greater if more productive manufacturing sources had been used.

Being dependent on other companies was not a position the Socony Petroleum Products Division enjoyed, and it was suggested that controlling ownership in the Cleveland Foundry be purchased to facilitate production. (In 1908 the Cleveland Foundry was already partly owned by Standard Oil, and was its main supplier of metal cans and containers to hold oil and kerosene.) There is no indication that this purchase took place.

Products marked "Rayo" were sold through general stores across the nation — outlets also for Socony's petroleum products. By 1924, as electricity became more available, sales of kerosene had dropped so low that it was no longer cost-effective to sell Rayo oil-burning stoves, lamps, lanterns, etc. Gasoline for automobiles was now the main product sold by Standard Oil.

A wide variety of styles of Rayo-marked lanterns are to be found, ranging from railroad styles and marine designs, to hot- and cold-blast domestic varieties. Some Rayo lanterns can be dated by comparing their style to the styles of other manufacturers found in this book and in the first volume of this series. When trying to date a Rayo lantern do not be misled by any patent dates on the lantern. Many of these precede the 1906 date when Standard Oil began selling Rayo. These dates are manufacturers' patent dates, some as early as 1894.

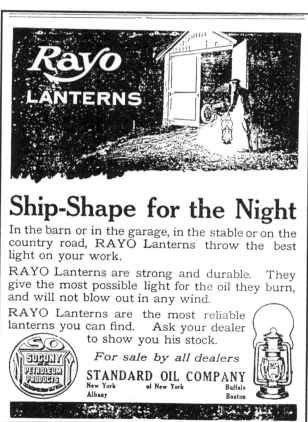

Ship-Shape for the Night

In the barn or in the garage, in the stable or on the country road, RAYO Lanterns throw the best light on your work.

RAYO Lanterns are strong and durable. They give the most possible light for the oil they burn, and will not blow out in any wind.

RAYO Lanterns are the most reliable lanterns you can find. Ask your dealer to show you his stock.

For sale by all dealers

STANDARD OIL COMPANY
New York   of New York   Buffalo
Albany   Boston

The lantern shown in this Rayo advertisement of 1914 is a Defiance Lantern and Stamping Company product.

The American Wick Company and the Standardization of Wick Manufacturing

Wicks were an essential operating part of the dead-flame, hot- and cold-blast lanterns discussed here and in Section II. As such, they could, and often did, reflect or influence some change in lantern design or technology.

Prior to 1760 manufactured wicks were round, and woven the same way as rope. During the mid 1760s, flat, woven cloth wicks became available. Flat wicks burned more efficiently than round ones, and gave a wide, brighter flame. Flat wicks were designed to be threaded through a metal tube held in a font and suspended in a fuel such as whale oil.

In 1782, Aime Argand invented a round, hollow wick, allowing fresh air to flow up its center. When used in conjunction with a glass globe, a greatly intensified light was produced. Within the next few years there followed an outpouring of new wick designs, each claiming to be superior. Consequently there were a variety of sizes, shapes, designs and materials, but no standardization — a situation which continued through most of the 19th century. Quality varied as well. All these factors could affect fuel consumption and light production.

Because of these variations in wick manufacturing, the trustees of the Standard Oil Company decided in 1893 to establish a wick factory to manufacture high quality wicks — in a large selection but with standard sizes and shapes. The trustees' reasoning was that if the public used better wicks — which used more fuel — the flame would be brighter and more consistent, and people would use lamps and lanterns more, therefore using more of the fuel sold by Standard Oil.

In a factory leased from Mount Ida Manufacturing Company in Troy, New York, the American Wick Manufacturing Company was established.

Because of their high quality material and accurate sizing, the wicks from this company gave much cleaner and brighter light and, as expected, led to greater fuel consumption.

Most lantern and lamp manufacturing companies purchased their wicks from American, knowing that fuel would flow evenly in these well-made wicks, giving a good light from their products. For example, Plume and Atwood, a very large manufacturer of lamps and burners, purchased more than twenty-six different sizes and styles of wicks from this company. By 1906 American Wick claimed they had the largest percentage of wick sales in the United States.

As electric lighting became more available, there was less need for wick lighting products, which caused a decline in wick demand. American Wick closed in the 1920s, having set the standards for wick manufacturing.

Today, wicks are still being manufactured as a miscellaneous product by various companies and available in many hardware stores.

Oil Containers

Many interesting containers — from small cans with or without spouts, to large five-gallon barrels made of galvanized steel, copper, brass, glass, or glass and wood, or any combination of these — were used to sell and transport illuminating oil. If you can find fine quality oil containers, they will enhance your lantern collection. The following illustrations indicate some of the many designs to be found on their labels and on the containers themselves.

Aladdin Security Oil was sold and distributed by Socony (Standard Oil) and had no connection with Aladdin lamps or lanterns.

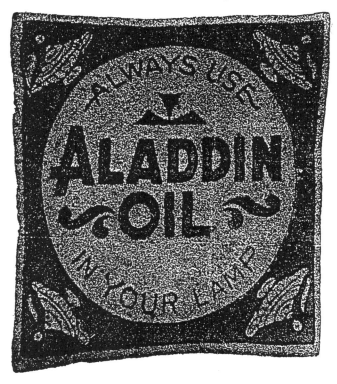

Felt Pad with Aladdin lamp motifs.

391

RENEWED

UNITED STATES PATENT OFFICE.

WEST INDIA OIL COMPANY, OF BAYONNE, NEW JERSEY.

TRADE-MARK FOR ILLUMINATING-OIL.

85,532.

Registered Feb. 20, 1912.

Application filed September 1, 1911. Serial No. 58,506.

STATEMENT.

To all whom it may concern:

Be it known that the WEST INDIA OIL COMPANY, a corporation duly organized under the laws of the State of New Jersey, and located in the city of Bayonne, in the county of Hudson, State of New Jersey, and doing business at Bayonne, in said State, has adopted for its use the trade-mark shown in the accompanying drawing.

The trade-mark has been continuously used in the business of said corporation since 1902.

The class of merchandise to which the trade-mark is appropriated is Class 15, Oils and greases, and the particular description of goods comprised in said class upon which said trade-mark is used is illuminating oil.

The trade-mark is usually displayed on the packages containing the goods, by placing thereon a printed label on which the same is shown.

WEST INDIA OIL COMPANY,

By WALTER C. TEAGLE,

President.

ALADDIN

DECLARATION.

State of New York, county of New York, ss:

W. C. TEAGLE, being duly sworn deposes and says that he is president of the corporation the applicant named in the foregoing statement; that he believes the foregoing statement is true; that he believes said corporation to be the owner of the trade-mark sought to be registered; that no other person, firm, corporation, or association, to the best of his knowledge and belief, has the right to use said trade-mark, either in the identical form or in any such near resemblance thereto as might be calculated to deceive; that said trade-mark is used by said corporation in commerce among the several States of the United States and also between the United States and foreign nations, or Indian tribes, and particularly with Porto Rico, Trinidad, Barbados, St. Thomas and St. Croix; that the drawing presented truly represents the trade-mark sought to be registered; and that the specimens, or facsimiles show the trade-mark as actually used upon the goods.

WALTER C. TEAGLE.

Subscribed and sworn to before me, a notary public this 2nd day of August 1911.

[L. S.]   A. T. DOREMUS,

Notary Public, Richmond County.

Certificate filed in New York County.

Page from the U.S. Patent Office Registry showing the Aladdin trade mark.

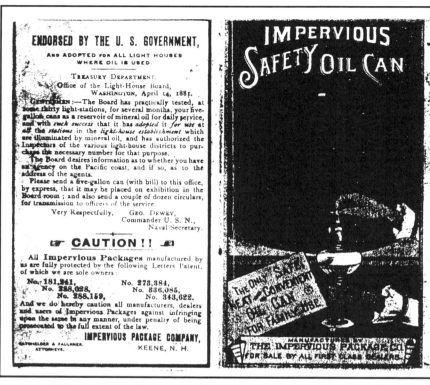

An 1886 advertisement for Impervious Oil, noting Commander (later Admiral) Dewey's endorsement of it for lighthouse use.

An advertisement for Impervious wooden oil cans with convenient spigot.

To the Trade and the Public.

ON passing into the sixth year of our business, we take pleasure in thanking you for your liberal patronage, and in again calling your attention to the record attained by our **Impervious Safety Oil Cans.**

Since 1883, we have made and sold over **half a million Oil Cans,** all guaranteed, and with claims for reclamation, amounting to less than one-quarter of one per cent., a record wholly without precedent in the history of oil carrying packages. This fact should be sufficient to convince dealers that our **Impervious Oil Can** is the most safe and reliable oil package to handle. But as the popularity of our goods has induced others to offer various styles of Oil Cans, most of which have **no safety or convenience,** we desire to call your attention to a few simple reasons why you should buy our Impervious Oil Cans in preference to all others.

1st. They are and always will be the best.

2d. They are absolutely safe.

3d. For the safety and convenience given, they are the cheapest Oil Can ever made.

4th. They are neat and attractive, and sell themselves when shown.

5th. No dealer can afford to sell an inferior article when he can give the best at the same price.

6th. We strive to secure all who sell our goods a fair and a uniform profit.

7th. They are fully protected by U. S. Patents, **and are the only Wood Oil Cans that you can handle without risk of damages for infringement.**

We fully guarantee every Oil Can we sell.

With a thorough knowledge of your wants, and every facility to meet them, we feel confident it is for your interest to place your order early for the Impervious Safety Oil Cans.

All Wood Oil Cans made by us, bear our name. All others are infringements.

READ OUR CAUTION

IMPERVIOUS PACKAGE COMPANY.

Proclamation of the superior quality of Impervious spigoted oil cans.

Below and on the next page are various trade marks used by the Standard Oil Company. Standard Oil manufactured a variety of petroleum products as well as lanterns and lantern wicks.

Trade mark registered by Standard Oil Company June 29, 1907. The word "gasolene" was also a registered trade mark of Standard Oil Company. Placed into use on July 30, 1907.

Trade Mark by Standard Oil Company. Design and trade name filed June 29, 1907. Used until 1917.

Trade mark by Standard Oil Company for kerosene. Filed April 25, 1907 and used for 10 years.

Trade mark by Standard Oil Company for kerosene. Filed May 1, 1907 and used for 10 years.

Registered February 1, 1906 for illuminating oil manufactured from petroleum. Placed into use April 10, 1906.

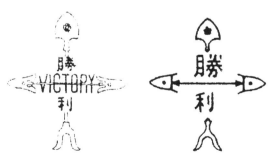

Two versions of a lamp oil trade mark filed July 1, 1905. An arrow, crossed with a double-head spear. The Japanese on the shaft is "sho-ri" (victory).

Top: Illuminating oil trade mark registered June 26, 1905. Bottom: Illuminating oil trade mark registered June 16, 1905. Both trade marks used until June, 1915.

Section II
Wick-Burning
Marine Lanterns

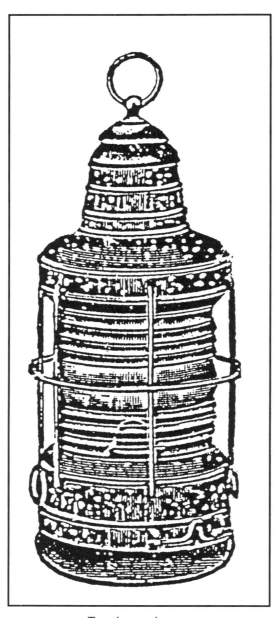

Typical marine lantern.

Marine Lighting Regulations

Prior to the United States ship lighting regulations introduced in 1910, lanterns for boats and ships had no size or design requirements. Because of this many marine lantern styles existed. After the 1860s, with the increased use of kerosene, the most popular style was the round-globed lantern made of all brass or all copper or a mix of copper and brass. The functional reason for using these materials was that brass and copper would not rust, and even with constant exposure to a wet environment, were far less susceptible to corrosion than were other metals. Aesthetically, brass and copper could be polished, maintaining an attractive appearance.

The pre-1890 brass and copper marine lanterns were usually far more fancy than lanterns manufactured for land use. It was common for them to have ruffled tops and ornate castings incorporated into their handles and hinges. By the late 1890s, however, the quality of galvanized steel had improved substantially and was offered as a cheaper but less decorative alternative to brass or copper.

In the 1820s Augustine Fresnel, a French physicist, had experimented with light refraction, producing a new design for a globe, turning it into a glass lens that would amplify the light shining from a lantern. These lenses were not commonly found on marine lanterns until the late 1800s, but after 1910 it was required that all ship lighting, with the exception of deck and signal lanterns, have these lenses.

The 1910 federal regulations also divided motor boats and ships of all types into four groups of size classifications. Class One was for boats less than twenty-six feet in length; Class Two, for boats from twenty-six feet but not over forty feet; Class Three, for boats forty feet to sixty-five feet; Class Four for ships and boats over sixty-five feet. Lens sizes were specified for each classification and varied according to lantern use.

Where known, these lens sizes for Classes One, Two and Three can be found in the marine lantern descriptions in this book. The lights required for Class Four were huge, are rarely seen, and are not covered here.

Class One light requirements were: a white light aft (rear); a green light on the starboard side (right); red on the port side (left), but located lower than the white aft light; all positioned so that light was thrown forward and to the side. The only size requirements specified for lights in Class One were that they be large enough to cover the purpose intended. It was suggested that the illuminated portion of the lantern be not less than three inches.

Class Two and Class Three required the addition of a "bright" white light in the fore part, as near the stem (front) as possible, and constructed so as to throw a light to the horizon on each side of the vessel. Combination lanterns shown in the following pages were a popular way to comply with this regulation.

Additionally, blue-lensed lanterns were used on tugs and barges to indicate they had something in tow. Lanterns with lenses or globes of one, two, or three colors (very often hand-painted) were trap lanterns, used by lobster and crab fishermen to mark their pots at night.

You can tell the class of boat it was made for by measuring the lens size (length and width) of a lantern.

Norwegian and British Regulation

Each country had its own laws governing ship lighting requirements. These laws were much the same for every country, except where the construction of lanterns was concerned.

The Norwegians and British had special requirements for their lanterns. Simply stated: "In the event of the glass, lens, or globe breaking, the lantern should continue to shine." This was easily accomplished by installing a

The "Cosmos" burner.

chimney on the burner. The chimney/ burner required by Norwegian laws was the "Cosmos." The British required the "Glass Cone" burner/chimney. American laws did not specify burner requirements but the "Vortex" was the burner most used in American ship lanterns.

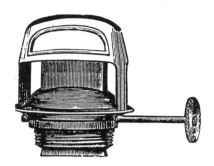

The "Vortex" burner.

The "Glass Cone" burner.

A secondary requirement for Norwegian and British registered shipping was that the lanterns used as masthead or anchor lights, be manufactured only of galvanized steel or all copper.

Anchor lights advertised by Perkins Marine Lamp Corporation. These were guaranteed to meet all requirements of British Board of Trade.

F.H. Lovell and Company
Lovell – Dressel Company

This company was founded by Franklyn Hallett Lovell, who was born in 1836 and spent his early youth on Cape Cod, Massachusetts. At the age of twenty-eight he opened an import-export business, F. H. Lovell and Company, on the corner of John and Pearl Streets, New York City. The main sales items were lamps and lanterns. One unusual lamp, in their catalogue for at least twenty years, was the Hitchcock lamp, which had an interesting clockwork system for maintaining a steady flame.

The business brought Lovell into contact with shipping companies and, to a lesser degree, railroad companies. He soon began manufacturing marine lanterns and lights as well as some railroad lighting. However, the railroad lanterns he sold were for the most part manufactured by other companies, such as C. T. Ham and R. E. Dietz.

In 1901 F. H. Lovell and Company moved their complete operation to Arlington, New Jersey, where it continued to keep up with new ideas and began to manufacture electrical lighting for ships and boats. Concurrently they manufactured oil lamps and lanterns for marine use. In the early 1920s F. H. Lovell and Company purchased the Dressel Railway Lamp and Signal Company, which had been started by George Dressel in 1882 in New York City. Because Dressel manufactured railroad lamps and lanterns, it was assumed that the acquisition would improve Lovell's position in the railroad lighting market, which proved to be the case.

The company changed its name to Lovell-Dressel Company and manufactured railroad and marine lighting and lanterns until 1967. Late 1968 saw the company purchased by Adams and Westlake. Lovell marine lanterns are marked "Lovell" on the bell top, and are pre-1920s.

Porter Company
Wm. Porter's Sons Company

William Porter, from Williamsburg (Brooklyn), New York, patented a design for a ship light in 1853. In the summer of 1862, Porter relocated his home and family to Manhattan. Within a year he opened the Porter Company, a marine lantern factory, at 271 Pearl Street.

During 1868 his son, William, Jr., joined the firm, and the company name was changed to Wm. Porter and Sons. In 1903 the company relocated to 67 Fulton Street and again changed its name, to Wm. Porter's Sons Company. In 1905 it moved to 23 Vanderwater Street, and in 1909 closed the manufacturing plant at this address. City records indicate that the company maintained an office at 241 Water Street until 1922.

Many lanterns manufactured by Porter's son at the Fulton Street and Vanderwater Street facilities were identical to the earlier ones manufactured by his father. The only difference was the name stamped on the brass oval tag mounted on the lantern. The earlier lanterns were marked "Porter Company." The later were marked "Wm. Porters Sons Co." Some very early Porter lanterns have no brass tag; the name is stamped into the top or side of the lantern.

Offered with Porter's marine lanterns was a small selection of railroad-style lanterns; there is some doubt as to whether Porter manufactured these.

Many Porter lanterns were distributed by Joseph Vogel, a firm located at South Fifth Street, Brooklyn. While Vogel's company manufactured some lanterns, it was, for the most part, a large wholesaler and distributor of marine lighting and equipment. In the 1916 Perkins Marine Lamp Corporation product line, there is quite a selection of Porter lanterns, indicating that Perkins probably obtained many lantern molds from Porter after the latter ceased manufacturing in 1909.

Improved Side Lantern
1903 – 1909

Finish: galvanized steel or polished copper.
Lens: Fresnel; 7 1/2" diameter, 10" high;
available in clear, red, blue, or green.
Dead flame.

English regulation, showing inner
chimney required.
Very expensive: galvanized steel cost
$40.00 a pair, and copper, $75.00 a pair.

Rare.

Improved Mast Head Lantern
1903 – 1909

Finish: galvanized steel or polished copper.
Lens: Fresnel two-thirds section; available
in clear, red, blue, or green.
Dead flame.

English regulation or, with top change,
Norwegian regulation. Also called the
Bow lantern.

Rare.

Seashore Lantern
1890 – 1909

Finish: polished brass.
Glass windows, with beveled edges,
enclosing chimney.
Dead flame.

The back door was galvanized steel, but
for 40 cents extra was available in brass.

Very rare.

Seashore Deck Lantern
1890 – 1909

Finish: polished brass.
Height, including handle: 11 1/4".
Glass windows; 4"wide, 5"high;
beveled edges.
Dead flame.

Price in 1900 was $6.50 each.

Very rare.

Improved Anchor Lantern
1903 – 1909

Finish: galvanized steel or polished copper.
Lens: clear Fresnel, 7 1/2" diameter,
10" high.
Dead flame.

English regulation. Could be special
ordered with Norwegian top and
German burner.

Rare.

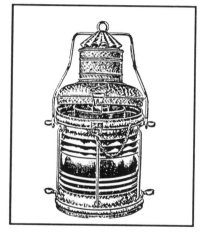

Ferryboat Side Lantern
1903 – 1909

Finish: galvanized steel, polished brass
or polished copper.
Two screw-in fonts.
Lens: Fresnel.
Dead flame.

Very rare.

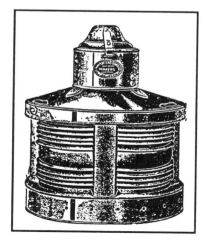

Bristol Brass Company,
Lantern Division

The Bristol Brass Company, Forestville, Connecticut, was originally a clock wheel and clock parts manufacturer. They purchased their lantern division in 1868 from a toy manufacturer named George Brown. Even though lantern manufacturing was only a small part of its business, Bristol Brass produced and sold a large quantity of marine lanterns in many styles.

During the First World War the Bristol Brass Company became one of the largest manufacturers of brass cartridge cases in the United States.

When National Marine Company became a lantern distributor in 1906, Bristol Brass supplied National Marine, located in New York City, with most of the lanterns they sold. Late in 1912 National Marine purchased the Lantern Division of Bristol Brass and reopened it as the National Marine Lamp Company, Forestville.

Bristol Brass Lantern Division lanterns are marked "Bristol Brass" on brass tags mounted on their fonts.

J. R. HOLLEY, Pres't, Treas. and Gen'l Mgr.   HENRY F. ENGLISH, Vice-Pres't.
ALEXANDER HARPER, Ass't Gen'l Mgr.   S. B. HARPER, Sec. and Ass't Treas.

THE BRISTOL BRASS CO.

MANUFACTURERS OF

Rolled Sheet and Platers' Brass, Brass and German Silver,

Rods and Wire Tubing, Brass Castings, Etc.

Bicycle Lanterns, Kerosene Oil Burners, Lamps and Lamp Trimmings.

POST OFFICE ADDRESS, BRISTOL, CONN.

Bristol Brass Company listing taken from a 1911 city directory.

H. A. J. Helvig

Established by Hansel A. J. Helvig in 1879, this company became a major importer of Norwegian sardines and Scandinavian fish and meat balls. By 1880 Helvig had started to manufacture marine lanterns, and soon had a manufacturing facility at 228 Pearl Street, New York City. He also supplied marine lanterns to other companies, and his products appear in catalogues of many well-known lantern manufacturers, including R. E. Dietz and C. T. Ham.

In 1905, the founder of the company died. 1906 saw the company reorganized and renamed National Marine Lamp Company. Helvig's executors closed the New York manufacturing facilities, but the company continued to operate as a marine lantern wholesaler and distributor at the Pearl Street address until 1923.

Lanterns manufactured by Helvig have "Helvig's" stamped into the metal or on an oval brass plate mounted on the lantern. Many of the Helvig lantern molds were later purchased by Perkins Marine Lamp Corporation.

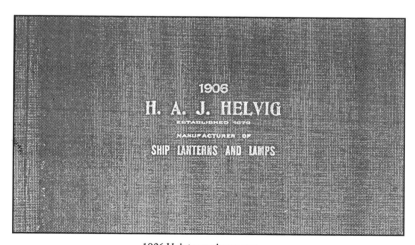

1906 Helvig catalogue cover.

Bow Lantern
1879 – 1906

Finish: galvanized steel or polished brass.
Six sizes offered, ranging
from 10" to 21" high.
Dead flame.

1879 – 1900 had clear glass;
1900 – 1906 had clear Fresnel lens
(shown). For an extra 20% of net price
the door could be moved to the side.

Very rare: all models.

Anchor Lantern
1879 – 1906

Finish: galvanized steel or polished brass.
Five sizes offered, ranging
from 14" to 23" high.
Lens: Fresnel, clear or colored (at extra cost).
Dead flame.

Bottom of lantern hinged down and font
screwed firmly into place.

Very rare: all models.

Fancy Anchor Lantern
1900 – 1906

Finish: galvanized steel or polished brass.
Six sizes offered, ranging
from 14" to 23" high.
Lens: Fresnel, clear or colored.
Dead flame.

Smallest size cost $7.50 each and the
largest $18.00.

Very rare: all models.

Side Lantern
1879 – 1900

*Finish: galvanized steel or polished brass.
Six sizes offered, ranging from 5 1/2"
to 10 1/2" high.
Clear glass front.
Dead flame.*

For an extra 20% of net price the bottom door could be moved to the side. Sold and packed in pairs.

Very rare: all models.

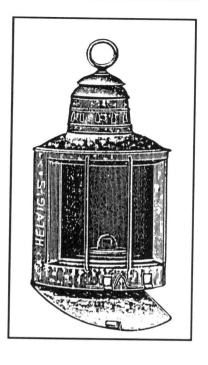

Side Lantern
1900 – 1906

*Finish: galvanized steel or polished brass.
Seven sizes offered, ranging from 9 3/4"
to 19" high.
Lens: Fresnel, in red, green or blue.
Dead flame.*

For an extra 20% of net price the door could be moved to the side. Sold and packed in pairs.

Very rare: all models.

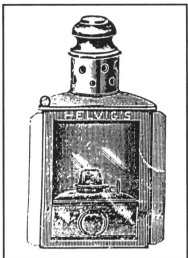

No. 54 and 55 Binnacle Lanterns
1879 – 1906

Finish: polished brass.

No. 55 Small:
Height: 8"; width: 3 1/2".
Glass size: 2 1/2" wide, 3 1/2" high.

No. 55 Regular:
Height: 9"; width: 4 1/2".
Glass size: 3" wide, 4 1/2" high.

No. 54:
Height: 10 1/4"; width: 5 1/2".
Glass size: 4" wide, 5 3/4" high.
Dead flame.

Binnacle lanterns were designed to slide into slots on the compass housing, and throw light onto the compass.

Very rare: all models.

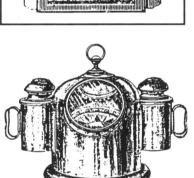

Binnacle heads (shown above) sat atop the stand holding the compass
on the ship's bridge. They held the binnacle lanterns.

Round Binnacle Lantern
1879 – 1906

Finish: polished brass.
Small: height 5"; diameter 1 7/8".
Regular: height 5 1/2"; diameter 2 3/4".
Large: height 6 1/2"; diameter 2 3/4".
Lens: round; clear glass.
Dead flame.

Very rare: all models.

Globe Lantern
1879 – 1906

Finish: galvanized steel or polished brass.
Globe: available in 6", 8", and 10"
diameter; ruby or green globes available
as special order.
Dead flame.

This lantern continued in the Perkins marine line from 1916 until 1925.

Rare: all models.

Fancy Hand Lantern
1879 – 1906

Finish: polished brass.
Globe: clear, red or green,
with bull's-eye lens.
Dead flame.

Bull's eye solidly secured to the wire guards.

Rare.

Fancy Engineer's Lantern
1880 – 1906

Finish: polished brass.
Globe: clear only; bull's eye added
to globe cost 50 cents extra.
Dead flame.

Price of lantern in 1900 was $2.50.

Rare.

Engineer's Lantern
1880 – 1906

Finish: polished brass.
Globe: clear only.
Dead flame.

A galvanized version of this was offered in the Joseph Vogel marine catalogue from 1890 to 1909, but not sold by Helvig, who manufactured it.

Rare.

Navy or Anchor Lantern
1879 – 1906

Finish: galvanized steel or all brass.
Height: 12 1/2"; base diameter 6".
Clear globes only.
Dead flame.

Hinged drop-down bottom; font screwed in.

Very rare.

Tubular Navy or Anchor Lantern
1879 – 1906

Finish: galvanized steel.
Standard with clear globe; ruby, red, blue, or green globes available at extra cost.
Dead flame.

The globe color "ruby" was 15 cents more than red, blue or green. This was because gold was mixed in to get the ruby color, while red needed only copper, which was not as expensive.

Very rare.

Combination Lantern
1879 – 1906

Finish: polished brass.
Lens: modified bull's-eye.
Dead flame.

New York pattern. Designed for launches. Price in 1906, $8.00 each.

Common.

Combination Lantern
1880 – 1906

Finish: galvanized steel or
polished brass.
Dead flame.

No. 1
Height: 8 1/2"; base width: 7".
Glass size: 3 3/4" wide, 4 1/2" high;
bull's-eye integral part of front glass.

No. 2
Height: 6 1/2"; base width: 7".
Glass size: 5 1/4" wide, 6 1/4" high;
bull's-eye integral part of front glass.

Chicago pattern. Designed for launches.

This lantern was probably manufactured by Joseph Vogel for resale by Helvig.

Rare.

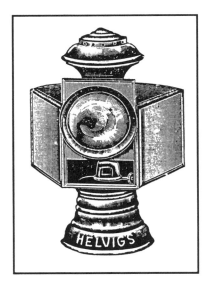

Combination Lantern
1890 – 1906

Finish: polished brass.
Height: 10".
Glass on sides: 3 1/2" wide,
4" high; 3" bull's-eye lens.
Dead flame.

Philadelphia pattern.

Available with a bull's-eye lens front
and back. Designed for launches.

Rare.

Combination Lantern
1890 – 1906

Finish: galvanized steel, or polished
brass, or some parts galvanized steel
and some parts brass.

No. 1
Height: 9"; base width: 5 1/2".
Lens: bull's-eye, 2 1/4" diameter.

No. 2
Height: 11"; base width: 8".
Lens: bull's-eye, 3" diameter.
Dead flame.

Boston pattern. From 1890 – 1900
polished brass only and the lenses
were not removable. Designed for
launches.

(Shown, 1900-1906 model.)

Rare: both models.

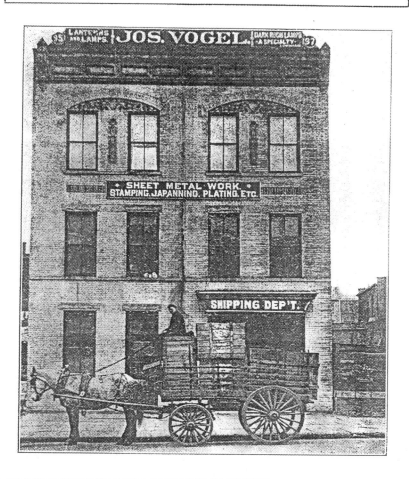

Catalogue cover for Joseph Vogel.

Joseph Vogel

Joseph Vogel started his company in the early 1880s. Located at 95-97 South Fifth Street, Brooklyn, he was a manufacturer, wholesaler and distributor of lanterns and marine products. He boasted in his catalogues that his "...immense stock would fill any order received." There is no doubt that he offered a huge line of marine products, but many of the lanterns in his catalogues were from other manufacturers, particularly H. A. J. Helvig, Wm. Porter's Sons, R. E. Dietz, C. T. Ham, and Bristol Brass.

Vogel lanterns are marked "Joseph Vogel" on an oval brass plate mounted on the lantern. What can be confusing to a collector is that Vogel ordered many styles of lanterns from other companies, and these were also marked with the Vogel name. It is therefore not easy to determine if a lantern marked "Joseph Vogel" was actually manufactured by him.

As a help to recognizing his products, take note of the handle shape on the Midget lantern (p. 87). This handle design appears to be unique to this company. Joseph Vogel closed in 1912. All the company's molds and equipment used in lantern production were eventually transferred to Perkins Marine Lamp Corporation. After 1916, Vogel-style lanterns can be seen in the Perkins product line.

Pearl Tin Oil Lantern
1890s – 1912

Finish: tin-plated steel.
Height, less handle: 7".
Clear globes standard; red, blue,
or green at extra cost.
Dead flame.

Advertised as the cheapest, best-made, complete oil lantern in the world. Useful for decorating yachts, motor boats, regattas and lawn parties. These lanterns cost $1.67 each in 1909.

Very rare.

Midget Anchor Lantern
1890s – 1909

Finish: galvanized steel or polished brass.
Height: 8".
Lens: Fresnel; 3 1/4" diameter, 3 1/2" high.
Dead flame.

The smallest Fresnel lens anchor lantern manufactured.

Rare.

Wizard
1890s – 1912

Finish: galvanized steel or polished brass.
Height: 8 1/2".
Lens: Fresnel or plain glass; 3" diameter,
4" high.
Dead flame.
Colored glass available at extra cost.

After 1916, Perkins Marine Lamp Corporation manufactured and sold this as the **Durable** lantern.

Rare.

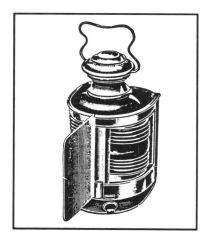

Durable
1900 – 1912

Finish: galvanized steel or polished brass.
Height: 8 1/2"; base width: 5".
Lens: Fresnel or clear glass; colored glass
available as special order.
Dead flame.
Hinged bottom with a snap-in fuel font.

After 1916, Perkins Marine Lamp
Corporation manufactured and sold this
as the **Wonder** lantern.

Very rare.

Baby Sailing Lantern
1880s – 1912

Finish: galvanized steel or polished brass.
Height: frame, 4 1/2";
base diameter, 4 5/8".
Lens: bull's-eye.
Dead flame.

Sold as a left side, right side, or bow
lantern.
Mounting bracket added as ordered.

Common.

Fresnel or Plain Boat Lantern
1895 – 1912

Finish: galvanized steel or polished brass.
Height: 8 1/2".
Lens: clear glass or Fresnel.
Dead flame.

Hinged base to access the font.

Rare.

Combination Lantern
1880s – 1912

Finish: galvanized steel or polished brass.
Height: 9".
Lens: bull's-eye in center, 3" diameter;
plain glass sides.
Dead flame.

For boats up to 26 feet. By 1916, Perkins Marine Lamp Corporation was manufacturing and selling this lantern, but with a Fresnel lens.

Very rare.

Combination Lantern
1880s – 1912

Finish: galvanized steel or polished brass.
Height, including handle: 10";
base width: 5".
Glass size: 2 sides, each 4" x 4";
round glass in center; bull's-eye available
at extra cost.
Dead flame.

Manufactured especially for canoes.

Very rare.

F. Persky & Company, F. Persky Company, Persky & Sumergrade Company, Perkins Marine Lamp Corporation, Perkins Marine Lamp and Hardware Corporation, Perko, Incorporated

Frederick Persky, who later anglicized his name to Perkins, was born in Russia in 1874. Schooled in Germany as a machinist and tool-and-die maker, he had mastered his craft by a young age. Armed with this knowledge he emigrated to the United States in the early 1890s, and was employed as a machinist by E. W. Bliss & Company, Brooklyn. Between 1901 and 1903 he and partner Joseph Sumergrade were operating a business out of a basement at 62 Elizabeth Street, New York City. This business was listed in the Manhattan corporate directory as F. Persky & Company, Machinists. There is evidence that in 1903 he manufactured "hand formed sheet metal items," "marine products," and "chartcases" at this address.

The company name was changed in 1904 to Persky & Sumergrade Company, at 49 Elizabeth Street. The company continued at this address until 1910, when it moved to 52 Elizabeth Street. Sumergrade lived at 49 Elizabeth Street, while Frederick Persky listed his home as Brooklyn. After 1911, Joseph Sumergrade is no longer mentioned as a partner while the name of F. Persky Company, Lantern Manufacturer, continued to be listed in the city corporate directory until 1913.

Sometime between 1904 and 1906 Persky received an order from a lantern manufacturer to make tool-and-die forms to stamp lantern parts. Who this manufacturer was has not been verified, but they did not collect the order. Rather than let these newly-made forms go to waste, Persky decided to use them and started manufacturing marine lanterns along with the other products he offered.

In 1907 his son, Louis, joined the company, and by 1912 they employed seventeen workmen manufacturing a wide range of marine products. They continued in operation at this address until 1913, when F. Persky Company closed. The building at Elizabeth Street was sold in 1915 to the Universal Metal and Stamping Company, also a marine equipment manufacturer and previously located at 145 Mulberry Street. Universal Metal and Stamping Company closed its doors seven years later.

Persky employees: July, 1912, at 52 Elizabeth Street. The person to the far right is Frederick Persky. The person in the far back, holding up the two lamps, is his son, Louis E. Persky.

In 1913 Frederick Perkins, formerly of F. Persky Company, became president of National Marine Lamp Company and moved to Forestville. He left New York City with the surname of Persky and changed his name to Perkins. In the spring of 1916 he left National Marine, and with his son Louis, started the Perkins Marine Lamp Corporation on Pitkin Avenue, in Brooklyn.

With Perkins Marine Lamp Corporation, at the same address, was Perkins Galvanizing Works. This division of Perkins hot-galvanized lanterns and iron items. Frederick Perkins, ever looking to manufacture the best possible product, could control quality by owning his own galvanizing works. Many advertisements from this time expound the virtues of this galvanizing process, as it protected iron from the corrosive ravages of salt spray at sea. During 1919 this galvanizing division closed due to major damage to the galvanizing vats, caused by negligence of the night watchman, who, instead of watching the heat regulation on the vats became intoxicated and fell asleep. The disastrous result was that the main vat cracked and then split, emptying its contents of molten zinc onto the floor and out into the street. This division was not rebuilt.

Over the next few years Perkins' reputation for excellent products became well known in the marine market. In 1931 the company name was changed to Perkins Marine Lamp and Hardware Corporation in order to reflect its now more diversified product line. The year 1932 saw great expansion and many more additions to their product line. This growth called for the building of additional manufacturing facilities. Five stories were added to their one-story building, and eventually they built or acquired six more buildings for manufacturing.

As the company's expansion continued, it ran out of space in the Brooklyn area. In 1960 it was decided to build a new facility in Miami. In 1961 the Brooklyn operation was closed, and all manufacturing was moved to one large modern building in Miami. At this time "Perkins" was dropped as part of the company name, which became Perko, Incorporated.

Frederick Perkins, the founder of the company had died in 1947, and his son Louis had become president that same year. Louis Perkins died in 1964, and his son, Marvin, assumed the top position in the company. Frederick M. Perkins, eldest son of Marvin Perkins, joined the family business in the late 1960s and is one of the industry's most knowledgeable people on marine navigational-light requirements. Frederick's younger brother, David, joined the company in 1981.

Perko continued to manufacture oil signal lamps and lanterns until 1996. They also manufacture all forms of ship lighting, including interior lights and searchlights. Lighting is only one division of the company. Included in their product line are many other items related to boats and ships. They are the only marine manufacturer producing high quality, die-cast bronze parts as well as sand-cast brass and aluminum parts. In fact, Perko manufactures all the parts for every item they sell, with the exception of small items such as light bulbs.

Sadly, we are seeing the end of an era as regulations and technologies have changed and oil lanterns and lamps are no longer required on marine craft. Battery-powered emergency lighting is now used. As a result, Perko is phasing out its oil lighting line, replacing it with the more advanced emergency lighting technology. In 1996 the last of their marine oil lights will be manufactured, almost 100 years after their first one was produced by Frederick Persky.

Lanterns marked "Perkins Marine Lamp Corporation" were manufactured from 1916 to 1930. It was in 1916 that the Perko trademark was registered and appeared on lamps and lanterns also marked "Perkins Marine Lamp Corporation." Some 1916 – 1917 lanterns can be found without the Perko trademark or Perkins name, but may have the patent date of "Jan 21 13" on them. Lanterns not showing the rays of light through the Perko trademark are definitely pre-1921. Starting in 1920 a trademark showing rays of light through the word "Perko" was used, and after that most Perkins lighting products were marked this way. From 1931 to 1961 their lanterns were marked "Perkins Marine Lamp and Hardware Corporation." Lanterns and lamps marked "Perko Inc." were produced in the Miami plant after 1961. Lanterns made by F. Persky Company prior to 1916 were, according to the best information now available, not marked.

Other than bridge lights, there is nothing to indicate that Persky or Perkins sold lanterns directly to railroad companies. Quantities of "Casey" lanterns were manufactured by Perkins and sold to the Keystone Company, which in turn sold to railroads. Other distributors and wholesale companies purchased Perkins lanterns for general sale, including Standard Oil (Rayo), Universal Metal & Stamping, Seattle Twine, National Marine, and numerous smaller concerns.

During the latter part of the 1980s, some fine reproductions of early Perkins lanterns were illegally manufactured overseas and put on the market in the United States. It is difficult to identify them as reproductions, because they look "antique." They can be identified, however, by the markings "Perko" and "Brooklyn NY" both stamped on an oval brass tag mounted on the lantern. Using this name was an outright trademark violation and most of these lanterns were pulled from the shelves of sales outlets. A few may have slipped through, so be on the lookout for them.

Vaclite Lanterns

Lanterns marked "Vaclite," either on the glass globe or on the lantern itself, were manufactured by Perkins Marine Lamp Corporation from 1916 – 1924. The term "Vaclite" refers to the fuel used by the lantern and not to the manufacturer. Vaclite is a flammable grease, of waxlike consistency, originally designed as a lubricant for steam and internal combustion engines.

Vaclite was produced by the Vacuum Oil Company of Rochester, New York. As early as 1877 the management of Standard Oil was purchasing Vacuum Oil shares. By 1879, with a $200,000 stock purchase, Standard Oil had acquired 75 per cent of the Vacuum Oil Company. By 1906 this company was almost wholly owned by Standard Oil. Vacuum Oil manufactured forty-eight different oils and lubricants. In the 1890s you could not go into a feed, general, or hardware store anywhere in the United States without seeing their products. One oil manufactured by them for automobiles at the turn of the century became famous and is still with us today as Mobil oil.

The market for Vaclite lanterns was the United States Navy and civilian marine users, as the fuel was spill-proof, even with the rocking motion of a boat. Railroad-style lanterns were used for Vaclite, being more stable than other lantern styles when set on boat decks. Though the spill-proof safety feature of Vaclite was useful, the fuel was inconvenient, requiring a special burner called a "Minot." The design of this burner allowed it to transfer heat from the flame down into the semi-solid fuel in order to maintain a fluid fuel flow into the wick, even with greasy fuels hardened by cold weather. Also, lanterns that used Vaclite were not as popular in the civilian marine market because kerosene and signal oil had more uses on ships and boats.

Lanterns for Vaclite were more commonly made of dipped or galvanized steel than of brass since steel was cheaper and sturdier.

Wax Burning Lantern
1916 – 1924

Finish: galvanized steel.
Globe: 3 1/2" diameter; 5 1/8" high.
Dead flame.
Manufactured to United States Navy specifications.
Operating instructions included with every lantern.

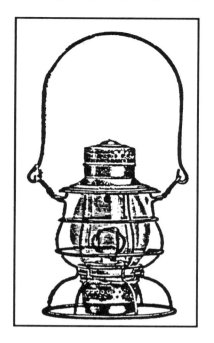

This lantern was manufactured with a round globe marked **"Vaclite"** on the glass, and sometimes the word **"Vaclite"** over the hinge on the bell top.

There were two styles of this lantern. The more common one (shown) had an open base and the other, a closed base. The lanterns marked "Vaclite" on the bell housing or glass also have a Minot burner, with arms suspended over the flame.

If the lantern is marked "Perkins Marine Lamp Corp, B'klyn NY" and "Jan.21.13" (the patent date), then it was made between 1916 and 1920. However, some of these lanterns may be found with no mark other than "Jan.21.13" stamped on them. These are still 1916 and 1917 manufacture.

After 1917, and until 1920, the Perko trademark, without the rays of light through it, was used on some of these lanterns. After 1920 they usually have the complete Perko trademark. The "Vaclite" markings were no longer used between 1922 and 1924.

The greatest quantity were manufactured between 1916 and 1919 for the United States Navy.

Rare: all models. But they are more often seen in coastal areas.

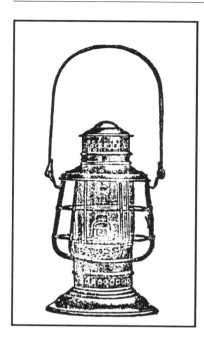

World Standard Deck Lantern
1916 – 1925

Finish: all brass.
Unusual straight-ribbed globe.
Dead flame.

Available with or without two brass rings mounted on base. A second version (not shown) was available with a moveable shield that slid up over the globe, to hide the flame. With this feature added it was called a **Dark Lantern.** Both types can be found marked "Dietz." These Deitz-marked lanterns were a special order manufactured for the United States Navy 1917-1918 for wartime use.

The navy was their main market, although some also were sold to the general public. A very well-made lantern.

Can also be found marked "Universal Metal Spinning and Stamping Company NY NY" or "Universal Metal Stamping Co. N.Y." Perkins sold them to this company for resale.

Rare: marked "Dietz."

Very rare: other markings or with tie-down rings.

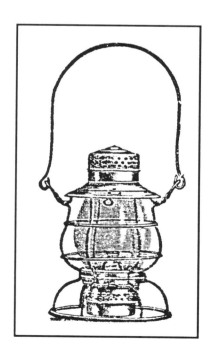

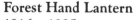

Forest Hand Lantern
1916 – 1925

Finish: tin.
Height: 10 1/2"; base diameter, 7 1/2".
Burned oil or kerosene, with different burners.
Globe: 3 1/2" diameter, 5 1/8" high.
Dead flame.

This same lantern, marked "Rayo," was sold to Standard Oil for resale. Common.

River and Lake Lantern
1916 – 1925

Finish: galvanized steel or all brass.
Height: 14".
Large convex or "B" burner.
Globe: very heavy quality, conforming
to government regulations; colored globes
available at extra cost.
Dead flame.

Price of brass version was $3.00.

Prior to 1906 manufactured by H.A.J.
Helvig, and then by National Marine
Lamp Company until 1914; by 1916,
Perkins had acquired the stamping molds
for this lantern.

Very rare.

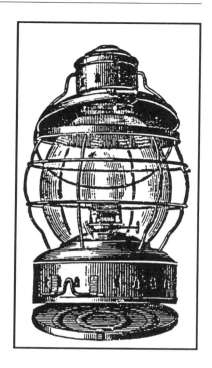

Improved Navy Lantern
1916 – 1925

Finish: galvanized steel or all brass.
Height: 12"; base diameter, 5 3/4".
Globe: clear; 5" diameter; 6 1/2" high; red,
green, or blue an option.
Dead flame.
After 1920: lantern height, 11";
base diameter, 5 5/8";
globe: 4" diameter, 6 1/2" high.

Manufactured on the style of the River
and Lake lantern but smaller, with
heavier guards. Approved for life boats.

Rare: both models.

Globe Lantern
1916 – 1925

Finish: galvanized steel or all brass.
Three sizes of lanterns offered, with 6",
8" and 10" diameter globes.
Dead flame.

Sometimes referred to as a "general" light. Lantern not usually marked, but the globe can be found with "Perkins" in raised lettering. Also called the **Signal** lantern.

Rare: all models.

Yankee Engineer's Lantern
1916 – 1930

Finish: galvanized steel or all brass.
Height: 9 1/2"; base diameter, 4 1/2".
Globe: 2 1/2" diameter, 4 1/4" high;
clear globes were most common, but red,
green, and blue available at extra cost.
Dead flame.

In 1916 these lanterns cost $2.20 each. Globe is sometimes marked "Perkins."

Rare.

Wonder Lantern
1916 – 1934

Finish: galvanized steel or all brass.
Class 1. Height: 8 1/2"; base width, 5".
Snap in-font, accessible through
hinged base.
Lens: 3" diameter, 4" high;
split color Fresnel, red and green.
Dead flame.

Combination light.

Until 1912 manufactured by Joseph
Vogel as the **Durable** lantern; by 1916,
Perkins had acquired the stamping molds
for this lantern.

Common.

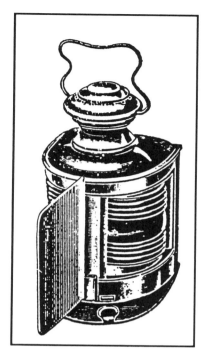

Durable Lantern
1916 – 1935

Finish: galvanized steel or all brass.
Class 1. Height: 8 1/2"; base width, 5".
Font is screwed into base.
Lens: 3" diameter; 4" high;
split color Fresnel, red and green.
Dead flame.

Combination light.

Until 1912 manufactured by Joseph
Vogel as the **Wizard** lantern; by 1916,
Perkins had acquired the stamping molds
for this lantern.

Common.

Wonder Junior Lantern
1918 – 1925

Finish: heavy tin-plate,
all parts screwed together.
Height: 10 1/4"; base diameter, 3 1/8".
Fuel: kerosene; full font lasts
36 hours on one filling.
Globe: clear, with colored globes
available at extra cost.
Dead flame.

Common: unmarked. Rare: marked
"Perkins."

Wonder Candle Lantern
1918 – 1925

Finish: heavy tin-plate.
Height: 10 1/4"; base diameter 3 1/8".
Supplied with candle holder only; clear globe
with colored globes available at extra cost.
Dead flame.

A useful lantern for every purpose: deck
parties, beach parties, lawn games, etc.
Rare.

Trap Lantern
1916 – 1929

Finish: galvanized steel.
Height: 13"; base diameter, 7".
Font: held sufficient fuel to burn 8 days.
Clear globe or Fresnel lens; 5" diameter,
6 1/2" high; color available at extra cost.
Dead flame.

Slight size changes in 1920, but lantern
looked the same.

Used by fishermen to mark their trap
line locations at sea.

Very rare: both models.

Trap Lantern
1916 – 1929

Finish: galvanized steel.
Font: held sufficient fuel to burn 8 days.
Lens: clear Fresnel, 8" diameter;
red and green available at extra cost.
Dead flame.

Also offered as a post or stake light.

Very rare.

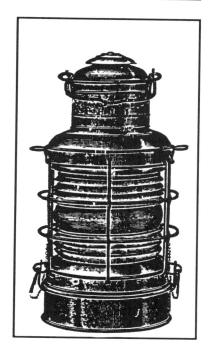

Bull's-Eye Lantern
1916 – 1935

Finish: galvanized steel or all brass.
Class 1. Height 9".
Screw-in font will not fall or jar out.
Lenses: 3" diameter, bull's-eye lenses
of two different colors.
Dead flame.
Three-way light to indicate "port,"
"starboard," and "clear ahead."

Until 1912, manufactured by Joseph Vogel; by 1916, Perkins had acquired the stamping molds for this lantern.

Rare.

Anchor Lantern
1916 – 1920

Finish: galvanized steel or all brass.
Six sizes available, to fit size and style
of boat:
Size 1. Height: 14";
*   lens: 4 3/4" diameter, 4 1/4" high.*
Size 2. Height: 15";
*   lens: 5 3/4" diameter, 5" high.*
Size 3. Height: 18";
*   lens: 6" diameter, 5 3/4" high.*
Size 4. Height: 19";
*   lens: 6" diameter, 6 1/2" high.*
Size 5. Height: 23";
*   lens: 8 1/2" diameter, 7" high.*
A small version was used as a stern light:
Height 11"; lens: 3" diameter, 3 1/2 high.
Clear, red, or green Fresnel lenses, all sizes.
Dead flame.
Turret Top.

Usually found marked "Anchor" in raised letters on the top. Manufactured by H.A.J. Helvig until 1906; by 1916, Perkins had acquired the stamping molds for this lantern.

Common: all models.

Improved Anchor Lantern
1916 – 1936

Finish: galvanized steel or all brass.
Sangster spring font, "B" burner.

Three sizes available:
Size 1. Height: 15 1/4";
        lens: 6" diameter, 5 3/4" high.
Size 2. Height: 16 1/4";
        lens: 6" diameter, 6 1/2" high.
Size 3. Height: 19 1/4";
        lens: 8" diameter, 7 1/4" high.
Clear, red, blue, or green Fresnel lenses,
all sizes.
Dead flame.
Hinged top and base.

This model may sometimes be found fitted for electricity. These were factory modified for special orders.

Common: all models.

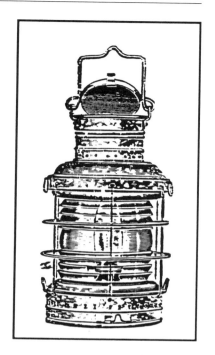

Little-Baby Lantern
1916 – 1955

Finish: galvanized steel or all brass.
Height: 8 1/2".
Screw-in font.
Lens: Fresnel; 3 1/4" diameter, 5" high.
Dead flame.

Left and right mount versions available.

Designed to use two lanterns in combination.
Until 1912 manufactured by Joseph Vogel; by 1916, Perkins had acquired the stamping molds for this lantern.

Common.

Stern or Anchor Lantern
1916 – 1920

Finish: galvanized steel or all brass.
Class 1. Height: 8 3/4".
Screw-in font.
Lens: 3 1/2" diameter, 3" high;
red, clear, blue, or green available
in plain glass or Fresnel.
Dead flame.

Until 1912, manufactured by Joseph Vogel; by 1916, Perkins had acquired the stamping molds for this lantern.

Rare.

Stern or Anchor Lantern
1916 – 1927

Finish: galvanized steel or all brass.
Class 2 and 3. Height: 14".
Lens: Fresnel; 4 3/4" diameter,
4 1/4" high; clear or colored.
Dead flame.

Rare.

Stern or Anchor Lantern
1916 – 1927

Finish: galvanized steel or all brass.
Class 1 and 2.
Lens: Fresnel.
Dead flame.

Originally manufactured by Bristol Brass Company and sold by National Marine Lamp Company until 1913; by 1916, Perkins had acquired the stamping molds for this lantern.

Rare.

Stern or Anchor Lantern
1918 – 1927

Finish: galvanized steel or all brass.
Class 3.
Screw-in font.
Lens: Fresnel.
Dead flame.

Also used as a towing light or riding light.

Very rare.

Improved Anchor Lantern
1916 – 1929

Finish: galvanized steel or all copper.
"Glass Cone" burner.
Lens: Fresnel; 7 1/2" diameter, 10" high.
Dead flame.

English Regulation. Available for electric or oil; fitted for both, $5.00 extra. Price in 1916 was $38.00 each, in copper.

Originally manufactured by National Marine Lamp Company; by 1916, Perkins had acquired the stamping molds for this lantern.

Rare.

Masthead Lantern
1916 – 1929

Finish: galvanized steel or all copper.
"Glass Cone" burner.
Lens: clear, Fresnel 2/3 section; 7 1/2" diameter, 10" high.
Dead flame.

English regulation. Available for electric or oil. A 2/3 section lens covered only the front and sides of the lantern, not its back.

Very rare.

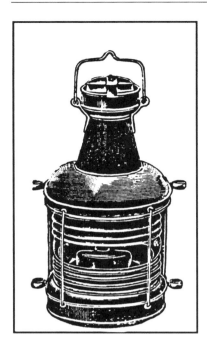

Masthead Lantern
1916 – 1935

Finish: galvanized steel or all copper.
"Cosmos" burner and chimney.
Lens: clear, Fresnel 2/3 section;
7 1/2" diameter, 10" high.
Dead flame.

Norwegian regulation. The "Cosmos" burner was a marine burner manufactured by Plume and Atwood Company, Waterbury, Connecticut.

Rare.

Anchor Lantern
1916 – mid 1930s

Finish: galvanized steel or all copper.
"Cosmos" burner and chimney.
Lens: Fresnel, 2/3 section "for maximum visibility".
Dead flame.

Norwegian regulation. Similar to the Masthead (1916-1935 model) lantern but marked "Anchor."

Very rare.

10 Day Anchor Lantern
1936 – 1950

Finish: galvanized steel or all brass.
Height: 14".
Font: 7" diameter; solid brass.
Lens: clear, Fresnel;
4 1/4" diameter, 4 1/4" high;
red, green, or blue available
at extra cost.
Dead flame.

A large, sturdy lantern, guaranteed to burn 10 days with good grade kerosene. Heavy brass hinge-hasp prevented font from falling from the lantern. Shown with font removed.

Common.

30 Day Anchor Lantern
1936 – 1950

Finish: polished copper.
Lens: clear Fresnel; 4 1/4" diameter, 4 1/4" high; red, green, or blue also available.
Electric.

The base held four 1 1/2 volt dry cell batteries, enclosed in a water and airtight container, sealed with a gasket and bolts. Guaranteed to stay lit for 25 to 30 days without attention.

Common.

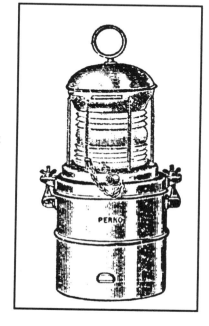

Open

Closed

De-Lite Side Lantern
1929 – 1960

*Finish: galvanized steel; polished brass;
brass, nickel plated or chromium plated.
Class 3. Height: 12 1/4";
base: 5 5/8" x 5 5/8", side to side and back
to front; weight: 4 lbs.
Lens: Fresnel; 5 1/4" diameter, 5 5/8" high.
Dead flame.
Turret Top.*

1937 – 1960 version shown. 1929 – 1937
style was slightly different, and can be
recognized by the rivets, rather than
screws, in the lens guards.

Common.

De-Lite Side Lantern
1929 – 1960

Finish: galvanized steel; polished brass;
brass, nickel plated or chromium plated.
Class 3. Height: 12 1/4";
base: 5 5/8" x 5 5/8", side to side and back
to front; weight: 4 lbs.
Lens: Fresnel; 5 1/4" diameter, 5 5/8" high.
Dead flame.
Flat Top.

Common.

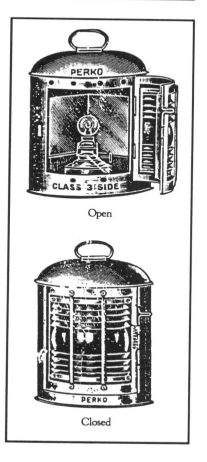

Open

De-Lite Stern Lantern
1936 – 1955

Finish: galvanized steel; polished copper;
brass, nickel plated or chromium plated.
Class 1. Height, less ring: 8 5/8";
base diameter, 4 1/2".
Oil font available with light bulb socket
attached.
Lens: Fresnel; 3/8" diameter, 3 1/2" high;
clear, red, blue, or green.
Dead flame.
Turret top.

Guards were fastened with bolts to body;
easily removed to replace lens.

Rare.

Closed

Font removed, with light bulb attachment.

Font removed, with light bulb attachment.

De-Lite Anchor Lantern
1936 – 1955

Finish: galvanized steel; polished copper; brass, nickel plated or chromium plated.
Class 2 and 3. Height, less ring: 11 3/4"; diameter at base, 5 3/4".
Sangster spring font.
Lens: clear Fresnel; 4 1/4" diameter, 4 1/4" high; colored lenses available.
Dead flame.
Turret top.

Oil or electric light, or combination, available at no extra cost.

Rare.

Bow Lantern
1916 – 1927

Finish: galvanized steel or all brass.
Hinged top and hinged "B" burner; all models.
Class 1. Height: 14"; lens: 6" diameter, 5 3/4 high.
Class 2. Height: 14 1/2"; lens: 6 1/2" diameter, 6" high.
Class 3. Height: 18 1/4"; lens: 8" diameter, 7 1/2" high.
Fresnel lens, all sizes.
Dead flame.

Price of the Class 3 in brass was $20.00 each.

Rare: all models.

Bow Lantern
1918 – 1930

Finish: galvanized steel or all brass.
"B" burner.
Lens: clear Fresnel, colors available.
Dead flame.

New design of font access for ease
in filling and lighting.
This lantern was designed to meet
specifications as a bow light,
masthead light, range light or a
stern light.

Rare.

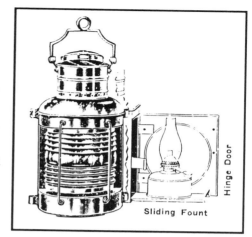

De-Lite Bow Lantern
1928 – 1960

Finish: galvanized steel; all brass; brass,
nickel plated or chromium plated.
Height: 12 1/4"; base: 5 1/2" diameter,
6 1/8" high; weight: 4 lbs.
Class 1 and 2: 1928 – 1960:
lens: 5 1/4" diameter, 7 3/4" high.
Class 3: 1937 – 1950:
lens: 5 1/4" diameter, 9 1/2" high.
Clear and colored Fresnel lenses available.
Dead flame.
Turret Top.

Common: both models.

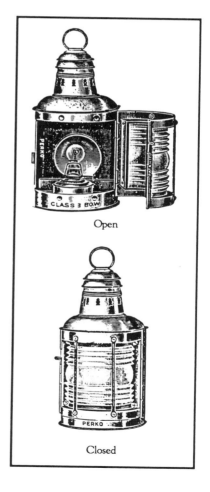

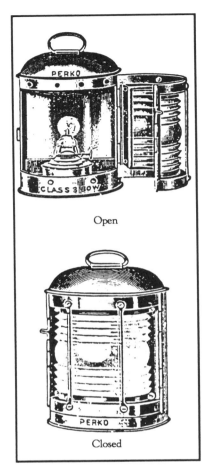

Open

Closed

De-Lite Bow Lantern
1916-1930

Finish: galvanized steel; all brass; brass, nickel plated or chromium plated.
Class 3.
Height: 12 1/4"; base: 5 1/2" diameter, 6 1/8" high; weight: 4 lbs.
Class 1 and 2: 1928-1960:
lens: 5 1/4" diameter, 7 3/4" high.
Class 3: 1937 – 1950:
lens: 5 1/4" diameter, 9 1/2 " high.
Clear and colored Fresnel lenses available.
Dead flame.
Flat top.

Common: both models.

Boat Signal Lantern
1916 – 1930

Finish: galvanized steel, painted black.
Several sizes were offered, from 6" to 12" tall.
Lens: bull's-eye.
Dead flame.

This lantern, sold by Perkins, is distinguishable from similar lanterns of other manufacturers by being clearly marked "Boat Signal" or **"Navigator."**

Also available was a flash version, also in several sizes, having an exterior lever that operated an interior cylinder which rotated to hide the light.

Common: all models.

Signal Lantern
1920 – 1940

Finish: all brass.
Lens: Fresnel; red or clear available.
Dead flame.

Although called a signal lantern, its
Fresnel lens and its very heavy
construction, indicate that this
lantern's real use was as an anchor
or masthead light.

Rare.

American Lantern
1916 – 1929

Finish: heavy galvanized steel or
polished brass.
Hinged burner and chimney.
Class 2. Height: 11 1/2";
base width, 10 3/4".
Lens: Fresnel; 6 3/4" wide, 6 3/4" high.
Class 3. Height: 13 1/2";
base width, 13 3/4".
Lens: Fresnel; 10" wide, 7 1/2" high.
Dead flame.

Used as a side light. Rare: both models.

Side Lantern
1916 – 1929

Finish: galvanized steel or polished copper.
Lens: clear Fresnel; 7 1/2" wide, 10" high;
green or red glass slides available.
Dead flame.

English regulation. For all classes of
boats. This lantern was sold in pairs, and
in 1916 cost $75.00 per pair.

Rare.

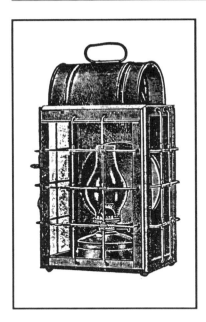

Standard Bulkhead Lantern
1916 – 1930

Finish: galvanized steel, all brass, or all copper; very often painted black.
Three sizes:
Size 1. Height: 11"; 7" wide, 7" deep.
Size 2. Height: 12"; 8" wide, 8" deep.
Size 3. Height: 13"; 9" wide, 9" deep.
Clear glass chimney enclosed in glass sides; bright nickel-plated reflector.
Dead flame.

Prior to 1918 only one side guard was used on this model; after 1918 an extra side wire was added. All the wire joints were reinforced with clips and double-soldered.

Common: all models.

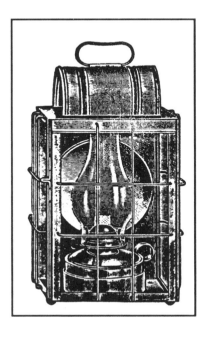

Popular Bulkhead Lantern
1916 – 1930

Finish: galvanized steel, all brass, or all copper.
Four sizes:
Size 1. Height: 11"; 7" wide, 7" deep.
Size 2. Height: 12"; 8" wide, 8" deep.
Size 3. Height: 13"; 9" wide, 9" deep.
Size 4. Height: 14"; 10" wide, 10" deep.
Clear glass chimney enclosed in glass sides.
Dead flame.

Guards were well-soldered to the frame but lacked the guard clips found on the Superior Bulkhead lantern.

Rare: all models.

Superior Bulkhead Lantern
1918 – 1930

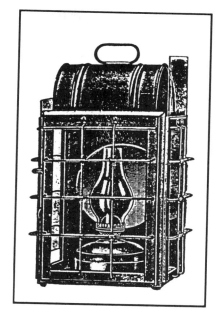

*Finish: galvanized steel, all brass
or all copper.
Large font and burner.
Three sizes:
Size 1. Height: 11"; 7" wide, 7" deep.
Size 2. Height: 12"; 8" wide, 8" deep.
Size 3. Height: 13"; 9" wide, 9" deep.
Clear glass chimney and large, heavy,
bright nickel-plated reflector, enclosed
in clear glass sides.
Dead flame.*

This lantern was made from extra heavy
materials. The guards were riveted, as
well as soldered, to the frame. Where
the guards crossed each other, brass clips
were added and soldered in place.

Rare: all models.

Chicago Style 3 Way Lantern
1916 – 1938

*Finish: galvanized steel or all brass.
Class 1: Height: 8 1/2"; base width, 7".
Lens: clear, bull's-eye, 2 1/4" diameter,
in center glass; red and green, 3 3/4"
wide, 4 1/2" high clear glass sides.
Class 2: Height: 10 1/2"; base width, 8".
Lens: clear, bull's-eye, 3" diameter, in
center glass; red, and green, 5 1/4" wide,
6 1/4" high clear glass sides.
Dead flame.
Combination light, with colors to indicate
"port," "starboard," and "clear ahead."*

Until 1912 manufactured by Joseph
Vogel; by 1916, Perkins had acquired the
stamping molds for this lantern.

Very rare: both models.

Boston Pattern Lantern
1916 – 1938

Finish: galvanized steel or all brass.
Class 1:
Height: 9"; base width, 5 1/4".
Lenses: 2 1/4" semaphores; clear in center,
red and green on sides.
Class 2:
Height: 11"; base width, 8".
Lenses: 3" semaphores, clear in center, red
and green on sides.
Dead flame.

Combination light, with colors to indicate "port," "starboard," and "clear ahead."

Very rare: all models.

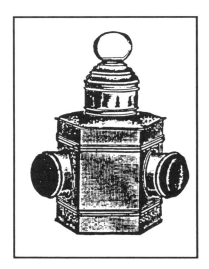

Boston Style Lantern
1916 – 1938

Finish: galvanized steel or all brass.
Sangster spring font.
Class 1:
Height: 9 1/2" ; base width, 5 1/4".
Lens: 3" diameter, round Fresnel
in two colors.
Dead flame.

Combination light. Font was inserted through the base of the lantern, but for an extra 75 cents a back door access was offered. Used as a bow light.

Until 1912, manufactured by Joseph Vogel; by 1916, Perkins had acquired the stamping molds for this lantern.

Very rare.

Chicago Style Lantern
1916 – 1938

Sangster spring font.
Class 1. Height: 10"; width 7";
glass sides, 4" wide, 4 1/2" high.
Class 2. Height: 12"; width 8 1/2";
glass sides, 5" wide, 6" high.
Plain glass sides only, in two colors.
Dead flame.

Combination light. Font was inserted through the base of the lantern, but for an extra 75 cents a back door access was offered. Used as a bow light.

Very rare: both models.

Ferryboat Side Lantern
1931 – 1960

Finish: galvanized steel, all brass,
or all copper.
Two fonts and two burners.

Two sizes available:
Small size: Height, less handle: 13";
base width, 14 1/2"; base depth, 10".
Lens: 6 3/4" wide, 9" high.
Large size: Height, less handle: 15 1/2";
base width, 17 1/2"; base depth, 11 1/2."
Lens: 7 1/2" wide, 11 1/2" high.
Separate red and green Fresnel lenses,
divided by a partition.
Dead flame.

Made from heavy sheet metal; cast bronze handle. All steel parts hot-galvanized after assembly. The brass and copper lantern versions are highly polished. For double-end boats.

Very rare: both models.

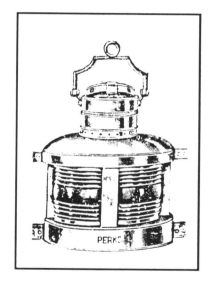

Pier Lantern
1937 – 1955

Finish: black nickel.
Height, less handle: 9 3/8";
base width, 8 1/4"; base depth, 7 1/2";
weight, 19 1/2 lbs.
Diameter of opening in top, 5".
Lens: 180 degree, ruby Fresnel; 12 1/2"
diameter, 7 3/8" high; green or red lenses
available.
Dead flame.

Cast from bronze.

Very rare.

Mid Channel Span Lantern
1937 – 1955

Finish: black nickel.
Height, less handle: 9 1/2"; weight, 22 lbs.
Lens: 360 degree, green Fresnel;
8" diameter, 7" high; red, clear,
or blue lens available.
Dead flame.

Cast from bronze.

Very rare.

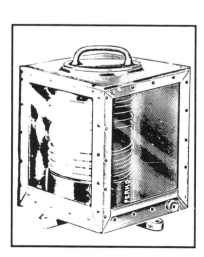

Drawbridge Lantern
1937 – 1955

Finish: black nickel.
Height, less handle: 11 1/2";
weight, 51 lbs.
Lens: 360 degree, clear Fresnel; enclosed by
two red and two green glass panels.
Dead flame.

An extremely heavy lamp.

Very rare.

Telegraph Signal Lantern
1916 – mid 1930s

Finish: galvanized steel or all brass.
Oil font with adjustable wick.
Dead flame.

This lantern had a moveable arm that opened and closed a shutter in front of the light. Mainly used by the United States Navy for ship-to-ship Morse Code signaling.

Very rare.

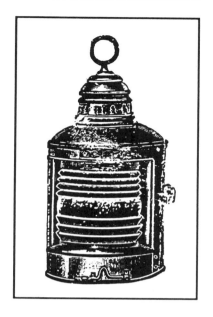

Telegraph Signal Lantern
1916 – mid 1930s

Finish: all brass.
Lens: Fresnel, 6" diameter.

Electric only; constructed with a special Morse Code key having heavy contacts. The base of the key held a condenser connected across the contacts to prevent arcing.

Very rare.

Torpedo Boat, Battleship and Destroyer Lanterns

It is very unlikely that you will come across any of these lamps and lanterns, as they were made for torpedo boats, battleships and destroyers in the First and Second World Wars. Rare.

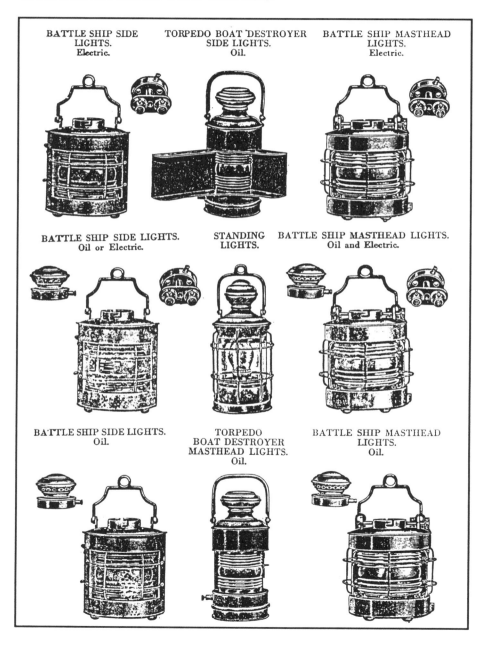

BATTLE SHIP SIDE LIGHTS. Electric.

TORPEDO BOAT DESTROYER SIDE LIGHTS. Oil.

BATTLE SHIP MASTHEAD LIGHTS. Electric.

BATTLE SHIP SIDE LIGHTS. Oil or Electric.

STANDING LIGHTS.

BATTLE SHIP MASTHEAD LIGHTS. Oil and Electric.

BATTLE SHIP SIDE LIGHTS. Oil.

TORPEDO BOAT DESTROYER MASTHEAD LIGHTS. Oil.

BATTLE SHIP MASTHEAD LIGHTS. Oil.

Catalogue No. 1, issued in 1916, by the
Perkins Marine Lamp Corporation.

National Marine Lamp Company

National Marine Lamp Company was established in 1906 as a reorganization of H.A.J. Helvig Company. A lamp and lantern distributor, National Marine's sales office was on Pearl Street in New York City. The majority of lanterns distributed by the company between 1906 and 1912 were manufactured by the Bristol Brass Company, and to a lesser degree by F. Persky & Company, and Joseph Vogel.

There are indications that at this time National was purchasing marine lanterns from Persky, Joseph Vogel, and, to a larger degree, from Bristol Brass Company. In 1912, National Marine approached the American Lamp and Brass Company, also known as the American Lamp Works, operating at 253 West Forty-seventh Street, New York City, and asked if they would be interested in forming a new company. The information is sketchy, but it

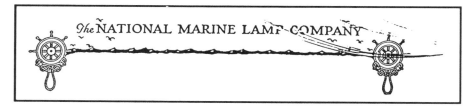

The National Marine Lamp Co.

Manufacturers of all styles

Lamps, Lanterns

Also Brass, Steel, Tin or Galvanized Iron Specialties
Galvanizing in all its Branches.   Write for Estimates

Brook Street   **Forestville, Conn.**

Two letterheads used by the National Marine Lamp Company.

appears that late in 1912 an agreement was reached between these firms and a new company was formed, keeping the National Marine Lamp name.

In the fall of 1912 National Marine purchased the Lantern Division of Bristol Brass. These buildings were located at 23 Brook Street, Forestville, Connecticut. National Marine manufactured lanterns at this facility and continued to maintain the New York City address as a sales office until 1923. Lanterns manufactured after 1912 by National Marine Lamp Company were sometimes marked with a 1912 patent date and/or the name "Triplex." This name referred to a special patented lens which could be installed on the lantern for a 10 per cent surcharge.

During the First World War, National Marine was a very large supplier of running lights and fog horns for the United States Navy, with 100 per cent of its output going to the military. By 1923 National Marine's manufacturing output was almost nonexistent, and on October 17, 1930, they filed for bankruptcy. In 1932 they reorganized as the Forestville Marine Lamp Company, at the same address. This venture was short-lived, and in 1937, the firm closed forever.

National Marine lanterns were marked "National Marine New York" on brass tags mounted on them.

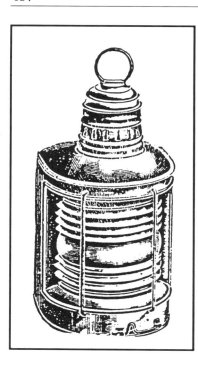

Navigation Lantern
1906 – 1914
1918 – 1923

Finish: galvanized steel, polished brass, or polished copper.
Screw-in or Sangster spring font.
Several sizes, from 13 1/4" to 20" high.
Lens: standard Fresnel or dioptric Fresnel; available in several colors.
Dead flame.
Bottom hinged to access font.

All sizes could be ordered with electric adapter for light bulbs. Used as masthead, towing, riding, and anchor lantern.

This lantern differs from the Side Lantern by its flat back.

Rare: all models.

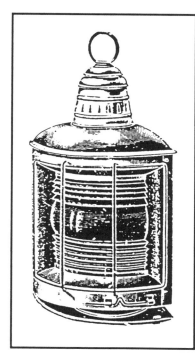

Side Lantern
1906 – 1914
1918 – 1923

Finish: galvanized steel, polished brass, or polished copper.
Screw-in or Sangster spring font.
Several sizes, from 13 1/4" to 20" high.
Lens: standard Fresnel or dioptric Fresnel; available in several colors.
Dead flame.
Bottom hinged to access font.

All sizes could be ordered with electric adapter for light bulbs.

The back of this lantern was not flat, but at an angle, so it could be installed flush on the side of the boat and still throw the light beam forward.

Rare: all models.

Other Marine Lantern Manufacturers/Distributors

Adams and Westlake (Adlake)

Adams and Westlake — whose history and lanterns are covered in the first volume of this *Lanterns That Lit Our World* series —manufactured railroad lighting as their main product, but many of their lights were used on barges and waterways.

American Lamp and Brass Company

American Lamp and Brass Company began manufacturing marine lanterns in the 1890s. In 1903 they were located at 44 Park Place, New York City. In 1905 they changed their name to the American Lamp Works, and in 1913 merged with the National Marine Lamp Company.

Boesch Lamp Company

In 1869, Boesch Lamp Company was established by Emil Boesch in San Francisco. Boesch was a lighting inventor. In 1892 the company was incorporated, with its address at 585 Mission Street. In 1907 their address was 1135 Mission Street. They closed in 1920.

Charles Durkee & Company

In 1903 Charles Durkee & Company was located at 3 South Street, New York City. In 1915 Durkee listed his business as a marine flag manufacturer. In 1920 he moved to Glasmere, Staten Island, New York, and soon afterwards opened an office in San Pedro, California. While he never advertised that he was a lantern manufacturer, his lanterns can be easily distinguished by the name "Charles Durkee" stamped on them, and by the use of rippled brass bands to hold the lens in place.

Robert Findlay Manufacturing Company

Robert Findlay Manufacturing Company's office was located at 28 Warren Street, New York City. The manufacturing plant was at 100 Lexington Avenue, Brooklyn. Opened around 1910 to manufacture sheet metal items and lanterns, the company was incorporated in 1916, and closed in 1921. They maintained an office at 224 Fifth Avenue, New York City, until 1924.

Howard and Morse Company

Howard and Morse Company operated from 1867 to 1898 from a factory in Brooklyn and a sales address of 45 Fulton Street, New York City. Included with its ship lighting line was a small selection of railroad-style lanterns.

Procter

Lanterns marked Procter's are named for Robert W. Procter from Clifton, New York. Procter patented an improvement to lanterns on May 16, 1876, but he was not a manufacturer. Who the patent was assigned to is unknown. Lanterns stamped with this name appear to have been manufactured from the 1890s to the 1900s.

Seattle Net and Twine Company

Seattle Net and Twine Company was a large Seattle-based marine distributor that later evolved into Pacific Marine-Schwabacher, Inc. Lanterns sold by them in 1916 were manufactured by Perkins Marine Lamp Corporation.

Nathaniel Tufts Company

Nathaniel Tufts Company was established in 1879. They had a sales office in Boston and a small factory in Charlestown, Massachusetts. Their name was changed in 1893 to Tufts Brothers. They continued to operate until 1902, with a sales office on Beverly Street in Boston. The main products manufactured were running lights and mast, anchor, and deck lanterns for ships.

Universal Metal Spinning & Stamping Company

Universal Metal Spinning & Stamping Company, also known as Universal Metal Stamping Company, was located at 52 Elizabeth Street, New York City, from 1915 to 1922. This company manufactured marine products, but lanterns marked with this company name were manufactured by Perkins Marine Lamp Corporation.

Wilcox, Crittenden & Company

Wilcox, Crittenden & Company, a marine lantern manufacturer established in 1847, was located in Middletown, Connecticut. They are still operating today as North & Judd Manufacturing Company. Their lanterns were marked "WC," with the C overprinted on top of the W.

Section III
Pressurized-Fuel
Lanterns

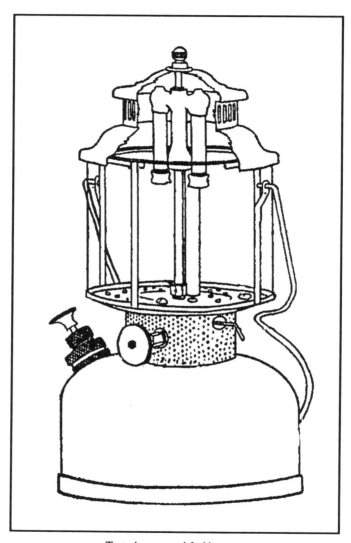

Typical pressurized-fuel lantern.

Development of the Pressurized-Fuel Lantern

Within the short span of two decades, from approximately 1890 to 1910, there came a great outpouring of inventions related to lighting. Between 1890 and 1900 the United States Patent Office received more than 2,400 patent applications for electric, kerosene, acetylene and other lighting devices. Discussed here are some of the patents issued for lamps and lanterns which used a mantle and burned gasoline, kerosene and other petroleum derivatives pressurized to form gas.

Many styles of wick-burning kerosene lanterns were available by this time, as kerosene was a convenient, readily available fuel, even in rural areas. However, the light from kerosene lanterns was not very bright. The invention of the Welsbach mantle, designed to be used with these flame-type lamps and lanterns, was the start of brighter lighting. Then an improved version of the mantle — for lamps and lanterns using fuel pressurized, by means of a small pump, to produce a vapor or "gas" which was then ignited — resulted in a revolutionary type of wickless lamp and lantern with an even brighter flame.

In March of 1898, patent 600,792, for a vapor-burning lamp, was granted to Arthur Kitson, a British subject who later lived and worked in Philadelphia. It had all the features of a modern day pressurized-fuel lantern except portability. Over the next few months following Kitson's patent there were many patents issued for similar but improved lighting systems. Among them was patent 618,078 (January 24, 1899) granted to A. J. English. His idea was to include a pressure pump built into the lamp font to replace the separate pump then in use. Another important idea came with patent 630,996 (August 15, 1899) granted to V. H. Slinack and assigned to the Pennsylvania Globe Gas Light Company. Unlike Kitson's or English's lamp, this one

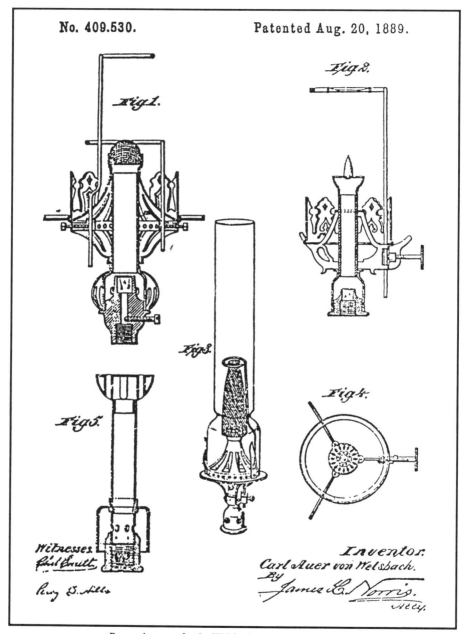

Patent drawings for the Welsbach incandescent gas lamp.

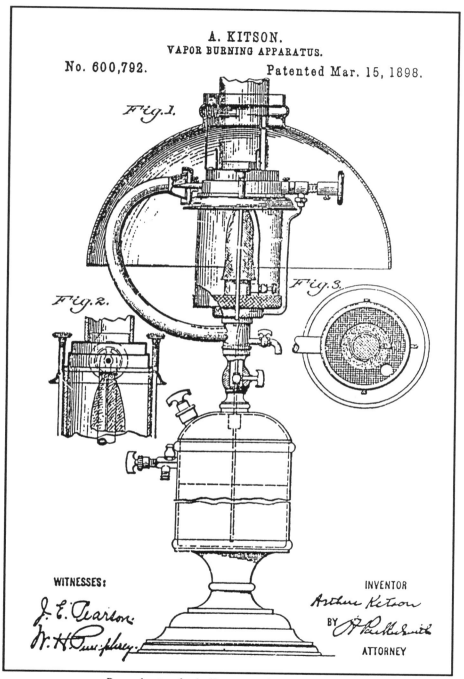

Patent drawings for the Kitson vapor burning apparatus.

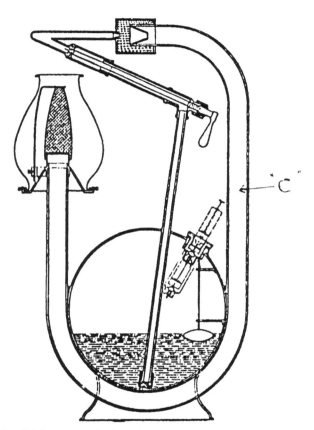

No. 618,078.   Patented Jan. 24, 1899.
                              A. J. ENGLISH.
                       HYDROCARBON VAPOR LAMP.
                        (Application filed Sept. 26, 1897.)

(No Model.)

"C"

The English lamp was designed to use coal oil or gasoline under pressure. Liquid fuel was forced into a valve chamber provided with a needle valve. When heat was applied, the vapor thus created was directed through tube C to the burner and mantle. Blackman assigned the patent to the Perfection Light Co. of Cincinnati.

Patent drawings for the A. J. English hydrocarbon vapor lamp.

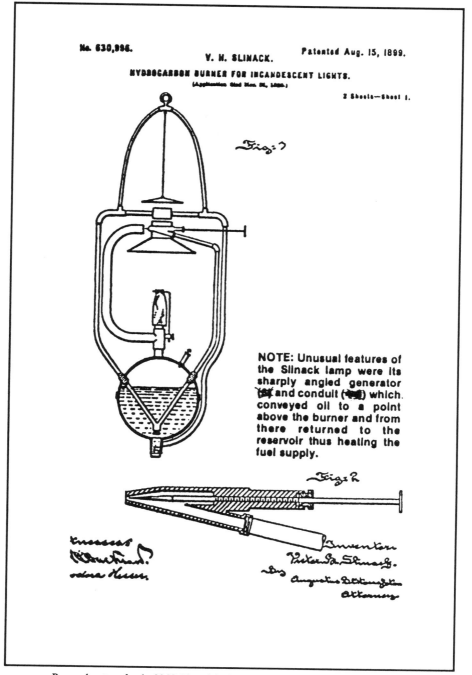

Patent drawings for the V. H. Slinack hydrocarbon burner for incandescent lights.

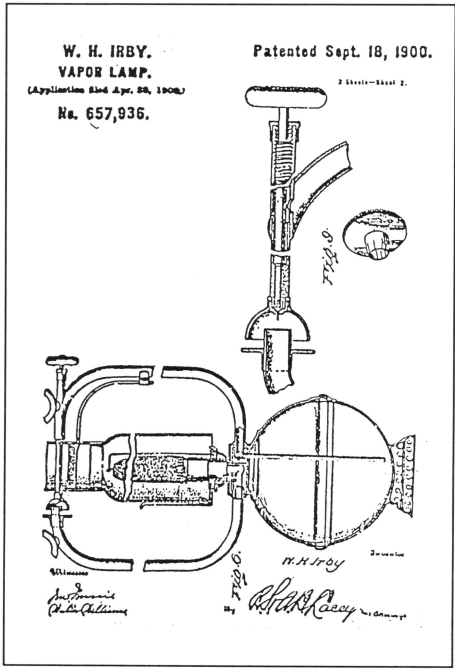

Patent drawings for the W. H. Irby vapor lamp.

was designed to be hung from the ceiling. Although it used the Welsbach mantle and Kitson system, it was held together with an unusual outside frame, which not only gave it physical stability and to some extent style and attractiveness, but supplied the fuel to the mantle.

These lamps were soon followed by one that, because of its portability and light output (up to 300 candlepower), had a huge impact on American lighting over the years following its invention. This was the forerunner of the Coleman lanterns we see today. The patent number for this lamp was 657,936, issued on September 18, 1900, to W. H. Irby. A pressurized-fuel lamp using gasoline, it was filed as a "vapor" lamp. From the patent application it can be seen that many details of earlier patents were incorporated into the design. In the application Irby stated that the object of his invention was "to improve the general construction through better assembling of parts, for better control of vapor and air."

Called the "Efficient," this lamp was manufactured in Connecticut by the Edward Miller Company from 1899 to 1903. From 1903 to 1907 it was still manufactured by Edward Miller and Sons but marked "Coleman Arc Lamp." After 1907 it was manufactured by the Hydro-Carbon Company, which later became the Coleman Lamp Company.

In 1913, W. C. Coleman patented the design for the "Arc Lantern." United States Patent office records indicate that no other patents for such a portable pressurized-fuel lantern precede Coleman's patent. Further, there is no evidence to indicate that other companies manufacturing lanterns at that time were producing anything even technologically close to the Coleman Arc Lantern. Certainly it was the forerunner of all portable, pressurized-fuel lanterns using gasoline. Thus we can say with reasonable certainty that W. C. Coleman was the first to invent and introduce such a lantern.

The Welsbach Mantle and Its Successors

Carl Auer Welsbach (1858-1929) was born in Austria. In 1885 Welsbach invented and patented a mantle for use with wick-burning kerosene or oil lamps and lanterns. The mantle was impregnated with chemicals. When suspended over a flame the vapors and heat from the flame caused a reaction with the chemicals in the mantle and created a brilliant light. Such light was called "incandescence," and all such mantles were called "incandescent" mantles.

The manufacturing method was to loosely knit cotton into a long "sock," then immerse it in a combination solution of lanthanum, thorium, zirconium and cerium. The brightness of the light the mantle produced

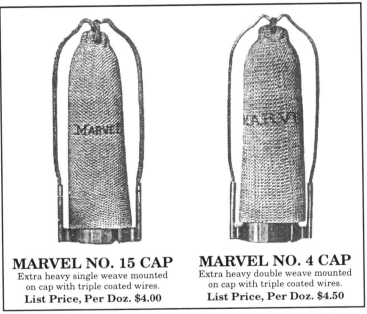

MARVEL NO. 15 CAP
Extra heavy single weave mounted
on cap with triple coated wires.
List Price, Per Doz. $4.00

MARVEL NO. 4 CAP
Extra heavy double weave mounted
on cap with triple coated wires.
List Price, Per Doz. $4.50

Incandescent mantles for wick-burning lamps and lanterns, advertised
by The Incandescent Light & Supply Company.

could range from bright white to soft yellow, depending on the amount of each chemical in the solution. After this immersion the sock was dried, cut into the desired length and sewn on the end, then turned inside out. After the mantle was shaped, a very hot flame was applied to burn off the underlying cotton cloth. The mantle was then submerged in a product called collodion, which gave it added strength.

Picture of Head Sewing and Tieing Department taken from early 1905 Incandescent Light & Supply Company catalogue.

In 1890 the American manufacturing rights to this mantle were purchased by the United Gas Improvement Company of Philadelphia. This company opened a division, called the Welsbach Commercial Company, to produce the mantles. This name later was shortened to The Welsbach Company. The company maintained offices in Philadelphia and its factory was in Gloucester City, Pennsylvania. The company produced a parlor lamp as well as a variety of burner assemblies to be used with their mantles. It was estimated that within the next ten years, ten million Welsbach mantles were sold in the United States. In 1906, the Westinghouse Lamp Company purchased the patent rights for the Welsbach mantle and became its main manufacturer. These mantles, which were for wick-burning lanterns, were not the same mantles as those used in pressurized-fuel gasoline and kerosene lamps and lanterns.

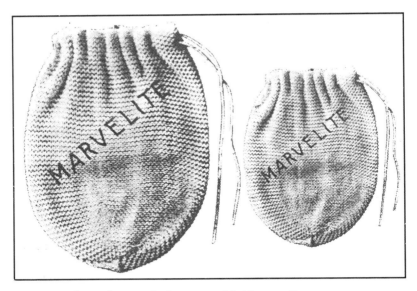

Inverted rag mantles for pressurized-fuel lanterns. From an
Incandescent Light and Supply Company advertisement.

In the 1900s, with the invention of pressurized-fuel lamps, there
came a need for a down-hanging mantle that would work under pressure. It
came to be called an inverted "rag" mantle. Unlike the Welsbach mantle,
which was designed to be suspended over a flame, the rag mantle was
required to be securely fastened to the lamp's gas outlet pipe, and to
operate without rupturing when the fuel was pressurized. Many
experimental designs were produced, but one outstanding design was
manufactured by the Alter Light Company of Chicago. This company,
jointly with Coleman's Hydro-Carbon Light Company, produced a
well-made, strong, inverted rag mantle. These two companies worked
together until the Alter Light Company dropped its mantle line from
production and turned instead to manufacturing light bulbs. A few years
after this product change the Alter Light Company became part of
General Electric.

During this experimental period in the early 1900s other
incandescent mantle manufacturers were producing reliable mantles for
pressurized-fuel lamps and lanterns. One was the Mantle Lamp Company
of America, which later became the famous Aladdin Lamp Company.
Another was a competitor of Coleman Lamp Company, the Incandescent

Light Supply Company of Chicago. The latter was acquired by W. C. Coleman in 1914, providing him with his own manufacturing equipment. The Coleman Company still manufactures rag mantles today.

Welsbach Company advertisement from around the turn of the century.

How Pressurized-Fuel Lanterns Operate

The pressurized-fuel lantern is designed to make its own vapor from whatever fuel it uses. Essential to the operation are liquid fuels (petroleum derivatives such as gasoline, kerosene, etc.), compressed air (via an air pump), a vaporizer (commonly called a generator), an air chamber, and a mantle.

The process begins by compressing the air and fuel in the font up to 40 pounds per square inch. This was accomplished on early models with a separate, hand-pressured air pump, while later models have a pump built into the font. The control valve is then opened slightly to admit some of the pressurized fuel into the generator. At the end of the generator is a small pin hole. The fuel bursts out of the pin hole into the air chamber as a fine spray or mist. There it mixes with fresh air. This mixture is now almost a gas, and as it enters the mantle it is easily lighted. When a match is applied the mantle initially tends to pop and flare until the heat from the lit mantle warms the fuel flowing into the generator, aiding

No. 242-K-905 Torch
For use with all Torch-Lighting Lamps and Lanterns
Retail Price, each..............................10c

No. 223-920 Bottle
For use with No. 242-K-905 Torch
Retail Price, each 20c

the vaporizing process. The valve is then opened all the way to allow unrestricted fuel flow, causing the mantle to glow and burn steadily. The lantern will continue to operate until its valve is closed or until it runs out of fuel.

In early pressurized-fuel lanterns, a process called "Torch Lighting" required, in order for the fuel to vaporize, that the generator be pre-warmed—by holding an alcohol-dipped torch against it—to an air temperature of 2,000 degrees Fahrenheit.

This was required because the quality of fuel then was not as good as it is today.

"Match Lighting," introduced with the advent of the "loop" generator, required far less heat to start vaporization. Sufficient heat could be applied to the loop area of the generator with one or two matches.

"Instant Lighting" needed no torch or matches or heat to start the vaporization, which was accomplished mainly via a redesigned generator (patented by Coleman in 1929), and by slightly increasing

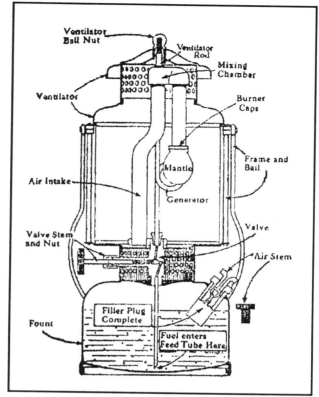

Illustration showing the technologically-advanced design of the Coleman Arc Lantern. The lantern was patented in 1913.

fuel pressure. Once the lantern was lit, the heat from the mantle maintained vaporization in the generator tube.

Pressurized-fuel lanterns using kerosene were more difficult to light than those using gasoline, because vaporization of this fuel was not accomplished as easily as with their gasoline counterparts. This problem was overcome by the placement of a metal cup around the generator tube. This cup was initially filled with fuel and then ignited. By the time the fuel in the cup had burned out, the generator tube was very hot and easily vaporized kerosene. Once lit, the heat from the mantle maintained heat on the generator. These cups surrounding the generator tube are a good aid in recognizing pressurized-fuel lanterns manufactured for kerosene use.

Note: Prior to being lit, any pressurized-fuel lantern should be checked by an authorized service person for function and safety.

Central Lighting Systems

The reader may be curious about the "lighting systems" mentioned in many of the manufacturers' history texts in this book.

The "hollow-wire" and "tube" systems of lighting were manufactured by American Gas Machine Company, Incandescent Light and Supply, Best Street Light, Acorn Brass, Economy Gas Supply, Nagel-Chase, Pitner, and many other companies. They offered a way to light large areas by using a system of interconnected lights rather than individual portable lamps or lanterns. In both systems, the fuel comes from one central source. In the "tube" system, the fuel is pressurized at that source. In the "hollow-wire" system, it is pressurized at each light.

The illustrations shown below and on the facing page and the accompanying text from a 1912 American Gas Machine Company catalogue describe both "tube" and "hollow-wire" lighting and show how they were set up in a dry goods and a hardware store.

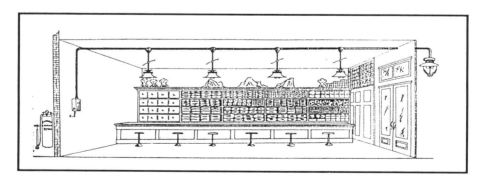

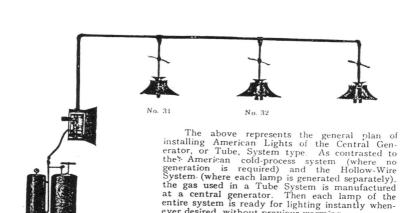

No. 31   No. 32

The above represents the general plan of installing American Lights of the Central Generator, or Tube, System type. As contrasted to the American cold-process system (where no generation is required) and the Hollow-Wire System (where each lamp is generated separately), the gas used in a Tube System is manufactured at a central generator. Then each lamp of the entire system is ready for lighting instantly whenever desired, without previous warming.

The principle of our Tube System is exceedingly simple, yet it possesses all the qualifications which go to make up a perfect apparatus. It consists simply of a generator and a reservoir, or tank. The latter is placed outside of the building for the purpose of storing the gasoline, which is forced under air pressure through flexible copper tubing to the generator located inside the building. The gasoline in passing through the generator is converted into illuminating gas, which upon leaving the generator passes through a mixing chamber into a Bunsen tube, where it is mixed with 95 per cent air to 5 per cent gas. This mixture is then carried through galvanized tubing throughout the building to the fixtures.

By the use of our Combination Tank, such as shown in the above cut, instead of a plain tank, a fresh supply of gasoline can be put in without releasing the air pressure or extinguishing the lights, should they be in operation at the time.

The lamps for the Tube System are of a different and somewhat simpler design than those for the Hollow-Wire System, and are furnished in a variety of attractive styles, as shown on the following pages.

None of the apparatus made by the American Gas Machine Company can be used interchangeably on *both* the Tube System and the Hollow-Wire System *except the tanks*, which alone are identical in style and construction for either system. Therefore, only Tube System fixtures must be selected for the Tube System, and Hollow-Wire fixtures for the Hollow-Wire System.

American Gas Company officers, 1912.

Factory and Office Building at Albert Lea, Minnesota in 1912.

American Gas Machine Company

The American Gas Machine Company of Albert Lea, Minnesota, was founded by Hans Christian Hanson, an immigrant from Denmark. Hanson was a blacksmith who settled in southern Minnesota in 1885. An idealist who believed he could bring lighting to millions of homes, he played a large part in the development of pressurized-fuel lamps and lanterns. The earliest lighting patents filed by H. C. Hanson go back to February 1, 1897.

Organized in 1894 and incorporated in 1903, his company soon had 250 employees working in what he claimed to be the largest manufacturing plant of its kind in the world. By 1911 it held a strong position in the pressurized-fuel lighting business, with branch offices in Memphis, Tennessee; Fargo, North Dakota; and Binghamton, New York. Early trade names on American Gas Machine lanterns included "Peerless" and "American." They also made wick-burning kerosene lanterns. American Gas sold their lanterns to other companies for resale, including Incandescent Light & Supply Company and Yale Light Company.

H. C. Hanson died in 1937, and was succeeded by his son Russell. This was a period of labor unrest in Minnesota. The Farmer Labor Union was very powerful and all American Gas Machine Company employees were members. A conflict began within the company over whether to change to the AFL's or the CIO's union. Oddly enough, wages and conditions were never in dispute, only which union they should join. As the conflict worsened there was a lockout. On April 2, 1937, the local sheriff and his deputies sought to remove the strikers, who were picketing. This turned into a riot and a police car was stoned and pushed into a nearby lake. Fifty-four people were arrested and jailed. Sadly, the company never recovered from the conflict and in 1940 filed for bankruptcy.

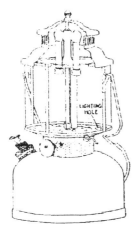

Workers at American Gas Machine Company, 1912.

American Gas Machine, which had been Albert Lea's largest employer, became part of the Queen Stove Works in that city. Following World War II, as a division of Queen Stove Works, American Gas Machine was still making pressurized-fuel lanterns, called "Kamplite." Production ended in 1968.

In 1935, American Gas Machine offered ten pressurized-fuel lanterns, all similar in style — with minor variations — to the lanterns shown opposite.

MODEL	SHADE	CHIMNEY	LIGHTING METHOD
101	Narrow	Glass	Instant
301	Narrow	Mica	Match – No tip cleaner
303	Narrow	Mica	Instant – Tip cleaner, inside access
3614	*	Mica	Instant
3606	*	Glass	Instant
102	Wide	Mica	Instant
302	Wide	Mica	Match – No tip cleaner
304	Wide	Mica	Instant – Tip cleaner, inside access
3618	*	Glass	Instant
3608	*	Glass	Instant

Model 3606 had a heavy duty valve control knob and a "Junior" mantle.
*Not known to the author at this time.

THE AKRON LAMP & MFG. CO.

EXCLUSIVE MANUFACTURERS OF

QUALITY PRODUCTS

592-606 S. HIGH ST.
AKRON, OHIO, U.S.A.

POSITIVE NO-RISK GUARANTEE
30 DAYS' TRIAL OFFER!

Important Message from
J. C. Steese, President

Dear Friend:

Your trial order for one of the amazing new Diamond 300 candle power lighting devices may be on the way to me, but if, for any reason it has not been sent in, I want to urge here and now that you delay no longer.

As told you in a previous letter, my offer of a new-type Diamond Lamp or Lantern at a special low agent's wholesale price, with an additional chance to get one absolutely without cost, could not be allowed to run on indefinitely. Now the time has come when I must set a time limit, after which the offer automatically expires without further notice.

In the first place, this is purely an advertising offer. Unless each Lamp or Lantern put out in this way produces orders for still more Lamps or Lanterns, I will actually lose money on each one. If I can get out enough sample Lamps and Lanterns in a sufficiently short space of time, however, I can be sure of a very gratifying volume of business. Otherwise, it is better to call the whole thing off.

So I must tell you that the chance to get your Lamp or Lantern on this liberal two-way offer will soon be past, as I cannot guarantee to hold it open more than 10 days longer. If your order is not received within that time, I may be compelled to give the opportunity to the next in line, for several others have written me about the new Diamond Lamps and Lanterns since you did.

It may be that you have been hesitating about sending in your order, feeling that perhaps my Lamps and Lanterns are not all that is claimed for them. If such is the case, I am now prepared to give you a guarantee that will positively eliminate all doubt from your mind. Read my double Guarantee Bond on the folder enclosed. You will notice that not only must the Diamond Lamps and Lanterns meet your every requirement in workmanship and materials, but that they must perform as represented by us, or no sale.

Furthermore, should you decide to try your hand at selling the Diamond Lamps and Lanterns, you are guaranteed a full refund of the deposit made on your own Lamp or Lantern after you have secured

(over)

Akron Lamp letterhead, 1930s, showing one of their lanterns,
(possibly the Diamond 300, mentioned in the letter).

Akron Lamp & Manufacturing Company

Established in 1898 and located at 592-606 High Street, Akron, Ohio, this company grew to be a large distributor and manufacturer of pressurized-fuel lamps and lanterns. They also manufactured pressurized-fuel gasoline and kerosene stoves, heaters and irons, as well as lamps and lanterns, and were a large supplier to such catalogue houses as Sears, Roebuck and Montgomery Ward. When they sold their products directly, they were sold under the "Diamond" trade name, and most were so marked. The lamps had a diamond design on the glass shade. The company went out of business in 1949.

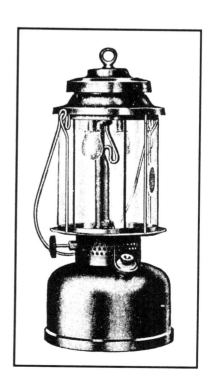

103G and 103K
1920 – 1943

Height: 14"
Fuel: 103G, gasoline; 103K, kerosene.
Font: 2 pints.
Chimney: mica.
Finish: bright nickel.

Ideal for motorists, farmers, merchants, fishermen, etc. This lantern is easily recognizable by its unusual, looped generator.

Rare.

Plant of The Incandescent Light & Stove Co.

Oakley, Cincinnati, Ohio, U. S. A.

Three Floors — 65,000 Square Feet Floor Space

Our new plant, located some eight or nine miles from the heart of the business district of Cincinnati. A modern, up-to-date factory building, equipped with every labor-saving device to facilitate the manufacture of "F-P" GAS MACHINES and "STUBBERS" lights.

Our goods are not sold under catchpenny guarantees, but the good will of every customer we consider a very valuable asset, and we do more perhaps than any other manufacturing house to deserve and preserve it.

Over 79,000 "F-P" Gas Machines, with Stubbers Lights, have been installed, and are in use in

Store Buildings of every kind, Warehouses, Railroad Depots, Churches, Court Houses and City Halls, Dwelling Houses, Lodges, School Houses, Factories of all kinds, Restaurants, Hotels, Saloons, Billiard and Pool Halls, Theaters, Parks, Gardens and Road Houses, Laundries, Tailor Shops, Vulcanizers, Linotype Machines, Laboratories and Barber Shops.

As to our responsibility, we refer to the Commercial Agencies, and we will arrange to furnish vouchers through any bank or banker in the United States or Canada, on request.

Geo. H. Paine

Treasurer.

Page from an Incandescent Light Company catalogue, early 1900s.

Incandescent Light and Supply Company

The Incandescent Light & Supply Company was located at 125 Market Street, Wichita, Kansas, with factories at that address between 1900 and 1914. They had sales offices in Denver, Oklahoma City, and later, a branch in Waco, Texas. They were manufacturers of pressurized-fuel lamps and lanterns and claimed to have made available to the public the first "low-pressure hollow wire gasoline lighting system." This was known as the "Marvelite" system.

Other products they manufactured were the "American Boulevard" arclight, a pressurized-gasoline lamp; the "Kerolite," a portable pressurized-kerosene table lamp; a pressurized-gasoline lantern; pressurized-gasoline automobile camp stoves, hot plates and water heaters; and the "Peerless" self-heating flat iron. There is evidence that they probably were a major distributor of American Gas Machine Company products while also representing other manufacturers of pressurized-fuel lighting products.

Incandescent Light & Supply Company also manufactured gas mantles, sold under the trade name of "Marvel." (See pp. 138 and 140.) This mantle division and its management seem to have been attractive to W. C. Coleman, for in the spring of 1914 he purchased the company, and transferred all of Incandescent's mantle-manufacturing equipment to the Coleman plant. Coleman later said he was more interested in the company's management personnel than its assets. Soon after purchasing the company he transferred Frank Reed and Charles Parr from Incandescent. Reed became Coleman Company secretary and Parr became general manager. The Incandescent offices in Waco and Oklahoma City were permanently discontinued during World War I.

There is some indication that Coleman continued to sell Incandescent's remaining stock of American Gas Machine products through the Incandescent catalogue for some time after the buyout.

No model number or name used.

Candlepower: 400.

Advertised as being useful for hunters, campers, construction gangs, lawn parties, miners, prospectors, etc. The only pressurized-fuel lantern they sold.

Quite an expensive lantern. In 1914 it was priced at $18.00.

Very rare.

Best Street Light Company

Located in Canton, Ohio, this company was operating by 1875, manufacturing oil and kerosene wick-burners, lanterns and street lights — the latter on the style of the Dietz "New York Street Lamp." R. E. Dietz mentioned Best in a note to his design department about other companies that manufactured street lights. In the early 1900s, Best started to change some of its production to the manufacturing of pressurized-fuel lamps using gasoline and kerosene. They also manufactured a number of pressurized-fuel outdoor lamps, the early ones bearing a resemblance to the Irby (later, Irby-Gilliland) design. By 1906 Best's lighting products appear to have been the gravity-feed type, where fuel drips down from above and into the lamp. They also offered a hollow wire system which used a hollow flexible wire to transport fuel from the fuel container to the lamp. The company apparently closed in 1915.

The author has not been able to determine whether Best manufactured pressurized-fuel gasoline and kerosene lanterns as well as lamps, although their lighting line contained such a variety of styles, including cold- and hot-blast wick lanterns, it would seem likely that they did so.

This advertisement for the Best Student Lamp appeared in the *Saturday Evening Post,* April 20, 1901.
It is believed that all Best lamps were of the gravity type.

Acorn Brass Manufacturing Company

Acorn Brass Manufacturing Company, located at 426 Clinton Street, Chicago, manufactured pressurized-fuel lamps and lanterns, hollow wire lighting systems, stoves and irons. In operation from 1900 to 1925, they marked their lanterns "Acorn." These have a very distinct, easily recognized, small inverted cup on their generator. When this cup was heated with a match, the heat was transferred to the generator tube.

Lanterns with private-brand labels were also produced by Acorn for mail order companies and hardware wholesalers, such as the "White-Lite" for Sears Roebuck. They also manufactured kerosene wick lanterns, marked "Uni-Lite." The Chicago Solar Light Company, also at 426 Clinton Street, Chicago, may have been part of the Acorn Brass Manufacturing Company.

350
1920 – 1925

Height: 13".
Fuel: gasoline; kerosene in emergency.
Font: 1 quart.
Mantle: Number 4, a special size.
Finish: polished nickel.

"Works well in extreme cold or heat."

Also called the **Uni-Lite.**

Very rare.

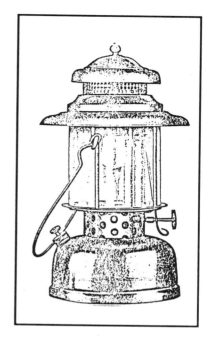

600
1920 – 1925

Height: 17".
Fuel: gasoline; kerosene in emergency.
Font: 2 quarts.
Mantle: used two.
Finish: polished nickel.

"A very bright lantern that can be used for street lighting, warehouses, parks, construction sites, docks, etc."

Also called the **Uni-Ark.**

Very rare.

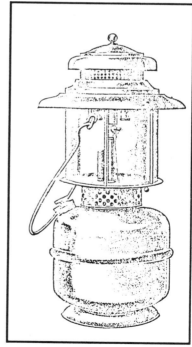

Sears, Roebuck & Company

Richard Warren Sears was born December 7, 1863, and died September 28, 1914. By 1886 he was working as railroad station agent in Redwood Falls, Minnesota, and in his spare time sold coal, lumber and other goods to town residents.

That year, a local jeweler refused to accept a shipment of watches sent by a wholesaler, as no freight had been paid on them, and they sat, uncollected, in the railroad storage building. Sears saw a chance to make some extra income and purchased the watches for a low price. He then proceeded to advertise them for sale and quickly sold his supply. He began to buy and sell more watches, which turned out to be a very good business.

In the fall of 1886 Sears terminated his employment with the railroad and established a mail order business in Minneapolis, called the R. W. Sears Watch Company. By the end of the following year he had moved to Chicago, and continued in an expanded business with the same name. At

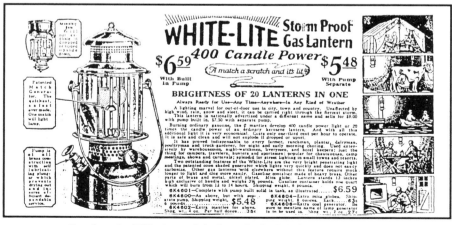

Page from the 1927 edition of the Sears, Roebuck & Company catalogue.

this time he needed a watchmaker to handle the repairs on returned merchandise and he contracted with A. C. Roebuck to do this.

In 1889 he sold his watch business for $100,000 and moved to Iowa, where he took up banking. Being a banker was not active or interesting enough for Sears, and the following year he returned to Minneapolis, again joining Roebuck, this time in a partnership in the mail order business.

When he sold the business in 1889, he had agreed not to go into the same business again in Chicago for three years. Therefore he initially operated from Minneapolis as A. C. Roebuck Company, which later became Sears, Roebuck and Company. Their first catalogue advertised only twenty-five items, but by 1895 it offered a thousand. The 1928 catalogue had many lamps and lanterns advertised, including a gasoline pressurized-fuel lantern called the "White-Light," manufactured for them by Acorn Brass Company.

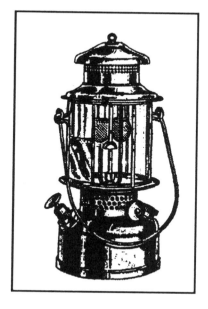

White-Lite

Candlepower: 400.
Fuel: gasoline.
Match lighting.
Available with or without a built-in pump.

This lantern was manufactured until 1925 by the Acorn Brass Manufacturing Company. It was still available in the 1928 Sears catalogue at a cost of $6.59.

Rare.

The Famous Pitner Lighting Systems

Pitner Gasoline Lighting Co.

Chicago, Illinois, U. S. A.

Code Address: Pitner, Chicago

Cover of Pitner Gasoline Lighting Company catalogue, 1906.

Pitner Gasoline Lighting Company

Pitner Gasoline Lighting Company's product line included street lights and other hollow wire lighting systems. The company operated from 1902 to 1915 in Chicago. M. W. Pitner, president and owner, authorized the writing of a combination training and sales manual for salesmen and prospective buyers that today remains as probably the most authentic and detailed explanation of the long-forgotten hollow wire lighting system. All the parts and construction methods are described in great detail, with an explanation of how each part functioned. (A copy of this training manual is in the Coleman Museum archives, in Wichita, Kansas.) While there is nothing in Pitner's product catalogue to indicate they sold pressurized-fuel lanterns, the size of their operation makes it plausible that they did so.

Economy Gas Lamp Company

This company was located at 122 West Seventh Street, Kansas City, Missouri, from 1898 until 1918, when it moved to 215-217 Goodrich Place. It is assumed that they also operated under the name Economy Gas Light Company at the same address, for apparently both company names were used concurrently.

In June, 1898, the company received a patent for a gravity-feed hanging lamp. The Kansas City directory indicates that this company offered pressurized-fuel lighting systems, as well as portable table lamps and kerosene wick lanterns. In 1919 they moved again, to 504 Delaware Street. In 1926, their last year in business, they relocated to 1701 Washington Street.

THE
NAGEL-CHASE
MFG. CO.

MANUFACTURERS OF THE

FAMOUS

REG. U.S. PAT. OFF.

and "DREADNAUGHT"

REG. U. S. PAT. OFF.

General Offices and Factory
252-260 EAST ERIE STREET
CHICAGO, ILLINOIS, U. S. A.

KEROSENE *and* GASOLINE LAMPS
and LIGHTING SYSTEMS

For the Illumination of Stores, Residences, Halls, Opera
Houses, Churches, Streets, Boulevards, Parks,
Wharves, Railway Stations, Etc.

Cable Address   Codes
   WIZARD   Lieber's   A B C 4th and 5th Edition
   CHICAGO   Western Union   Private

1919

Exclusive Agencies to Responsible
Parties in All Parts of the World

WRITE FOR PRICE LIST

The Largest Manufacturers of Artificial
Lighting Devices in the World

Nagel-Chase Manufacturing Company catalogue cover, 1919.

Nagel-Chase Manufacturing Company

Nagel-Chase Manufacturing Company, with Theodore Nagel as president and Guy Chase as secretary-treasurer, was located at 154-166 East Erie Street, Chicago, from 1904 to 1913. They then moved to 252-260 East Erie Street, where they remained through the 1920s. This company was one of the larger manufacturers of gasoline and kerosene lighting systems, lamps and pressurized-fuel lanterns. Names commonly found on their lamps and lanterns are "Dreadnaught" and "Quik-lit." The name "Wizard" can be found on their hollow wire lighting systems, such as street lights.

KEROSENE
AND
GASOLINE
LANTERNS

Absolutely bug and wind proof and give 300 candle power of light, at a cost of $\frac{1}{8}$c per hour. Suitable for use on farms, watchmen, side shows, circuses, street carnivals, garages, livery barns, summer resorts, warehouses, boat landings, etc.

For complete catalog and agency proposition address

THE NAGEL-CHASE MFG. CO.
150 East Erie St.   CHICAGO

Circa 1910 advertisement for Nagel-Chase lanterns.

THEODORE NAGEL, Pres   JOSEPH GRANZ, Genl Supt   A G RADOMSKI Sales Mgr   GUY M CHASE Secy & Treas

ALL ORDERS AND CONTRACTS ARE ACCEPTED SUBJECT TO STRIKES ACCIDENTS OR DELAYS BEYOND OUR CONTROL

THE NAGEL-CHASE MFG. CO.

MANUFACTURERS OF THE

Wizard

REG. U.S. PATENT OFFICE.

THE INSTANTANEOUS

CABLE ADDRESS
"WIZARD CHICAGO"

CODES { WESTERN UNION
A B C 4TH & 5TH EDITION
LIEBERS AND
PRIVATE }

TELEPHONES
DEARBORN 56
" 57

HYDRO-CARBON LIGHTING SYSTEMS

GENERAL OFFICES AND FACTORY
154-166 EAST ERIE ST. (ST. CLAIR BLDG.)

CHICAGO, Oct. 1st, 1913.

Dear Sir:-

Enclosed herewith you will find a copy of our 1913-14 catalog, in which we illustrate and describe several new inventions in artificial lighting. We trust that you will look over this catalog very carefully, as we are confident that after you have done so, you will admit that we now have a line that is second to none, and which will enable you to do a very nice business in your territory this coming season, if you are interested in representing us as our agent.

The KEROSENE lamps and systems, we especially call to your attention, because same are an achievement, surpassing all other known methods of artificial lighting. Outside of the fact that KEROSENE costs considerably less than GASOLINE, a gallon of this fuel will last about 35% longer than a gallon of gasoline, which makes the cost of operating a lamp, rated at 500 candle power, about 1/9¢ per hour.

The "DREADNAUGHT" type of KEROSENE lamp, on account of its attractive appearance, the enamel body and the more even distribution of light, we know will be the lamp, for which there will be the greatest demand, although we assure you the other styles can also be relied upon to give the same satisfaction.

The "DREADNAUGHT" and "QUICKLIT" GASOLINE lamps are absolutely the most perfect and up-to-date GASOLINE lamps ever put on the market, as same can be relied upon to give absolute satisfaction, even though put into the hands of people who are not familiar with artificial lighting, and also where good clean gasoline is not always obtainable.

We trust that the above will have your attention, and that we will hear from you if you are interested in purchasing a lighting system or taking hold of an agency for the exclusive sale of our goods in your territory.

Yours truly,
THE NAGEL CHASE MFG. CO.

Per _____
Sales Manager.

AGR/AGF

1913 Nagel-Chase letterhead.

Number 4
1919

Candle power: 300.
Fuel: kerosene.
Chimney: mica.
Finish: unknown, but probably bright nickel.

Self cleaning generator; separate hand pump.

Very rare.

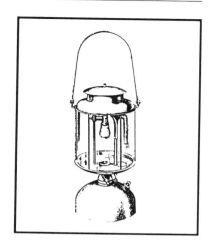

No model number or name used.

Candlepower: 300.

One of these lanterns was for gasoline, the other for kerosene. It is not known when these were manufactured. Their style suggests the 1920's.

Very rare.

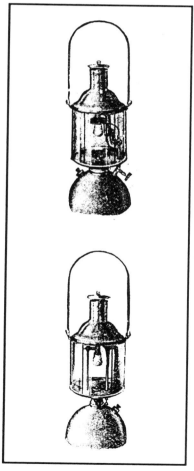

CATALOG No. 57

"KERO SAFE"
TRADE MARK

KEROSENE (COAL OIL)
SPECIALTIES

THE LIGHT OF THE HOME

LAMPS AND LANTERNS

THE THOMAS MANUFACTURING COMPANY

MANUFACTURERS AND SOLE DISTRIBUTORS   DAYTON, OHIO

Circa 1918 catalogue cover for Thomas Manufacturing Company.

Thomas Manufacturing Company

Located in Dayton, Ohio, Thomas Manufacturing Company was established in 1908, making phonograph motors, phonograph parts and general merchandise.

Lighting appears to have become part of their line around 1914. Soon thereafter they offered a torch lighting, pressurized-fuel lantern using kerosene, although this was at a time when the pressurized-fuel lantern using gasoline was rising in popularity. (Pressurized-kerosene lanterns were perhaps safer than pressurized-gasoline lanterns, and gave good light — up to 300 candlepower— although they were not as reliable as the gasoline lanterns under adverse storm conditions.) The trade name for this company's lanterns was "KeroSafe." Thomas Manufacturing Company closed its doors at the end of 1926.

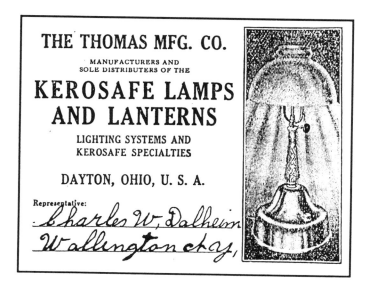

Explode or Set Fire to   Putting Up the Horse   In the House
       Anything

The KeroSafe Lantern

No Wick, No Smoke, No Dirt, No Grease, No Mantle Trouble, No Danger

The KeroSafe Outdoor Lamp and Hand Lantern gives a 300 candle power light that surpasses all imagination. You should see it burning at night to appreciate what a wonderful light it really gives. It makes the ordinary lantern look like a candle. There is actually no comparison with the KeroSafe. Night is turned into day. Night work is easy with the KeroSafe, for it throws out a 300 candle power light in every direction that scatters darkness almost as effectually as the sun itself. The KeroSafe lantern has all the advantages of the KeroSafe lamp, but the special advantage of the lantern is

Safety First

The most important consideration in buying a lantern is safety. The KeroSafe, as its name implies, was designed with safety as its principal aim. The lantern is so constructed that only a tiny amount of coal oil vapor, is supplied to the burner at a time, the supply feed being only 6-1000 of an inch in diameter. The KeroSafe is the only lantern on the market that successfully burns kerosene. It can't explode. As a further protection, it is fitted with a Mica Chimney that prevents the flame from igniting anything near it. If the KeroSafe were to fall among rags or into a lot of paper or hay, it would do no damage. It can't set fire to anything. If it were accidentally upset it would continue to burn. IT WOULD NOT EXPLODE.

Mantle Durability

The KeroSafe Mantles are the most durable mantles it is possible to get. Before they are used they may be handled without injury. Even after being burnt off they are much less fragile than the ordinary mantle. With our shade arrangement, the mantles are rendered much more durable than they are without shade. The lantern may be swung about as vigorously as an ordinary lantern without danger of breaking the mantles. This feature makes it especially desirable for trainmen for signaling purposes. They can swing the KeroSafe aloft, turning it over and over. The lantern keeps on burning and the mantles will not break.

Splendid Outdoor Light

The Mica Globe makes the KeroSafe the ideal outdoor light. Indoors it is a very satisfactory light, as windows and doors may be thrown open at will. Draughts have no effect on a KeroSafe. For outdoors affairs it is just the thing. Bugs and insects cannot get at the mantles and break them.

As a Street Lamp

Another splendid feature of the KeroSafe Lantern is that it can be used as a street lamp. Hung up on a pole at a street corner it will give as much light as an arc light. Every village and town not equipped with electric lights should buy these KeroSafe Outdoor Lamps, one for each street corner.

Circa 1920 advertisement for KeroSafe lantern.

M-1004

1920 – 1926

Height: 14".
Fuel: kerosene.
Font: 6" diameter.
Chimney: mica, 5" high by 5" diameter.
Finish: nickel plated.

Also called the **KeroSafe.**

Designed for use by ranchmen, night watchmen, plumbers, circus shows, etc.

Very rare.

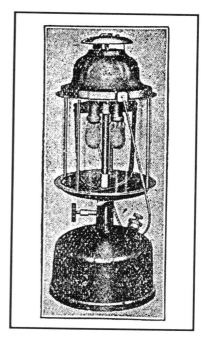

M-1011

Red Light Attachment.

Ideal vehicle light attachment, consisting of a shield with a red bull's-eye lens, that fit over the M-1004 lantern. Gave a clear, bright white light forward and a red light to the rear.

Very rare.

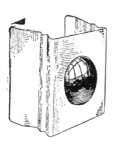

Sunshine Safety Lamp Company

The Sunshine Safety Lamp Company, established in 1910, operated in Kansas City, Missouri. They were distributors, and possibly manufacturers. In 1914, they purchased from the Coleman Lamp Company its new "Arc" lantern and in 1917 bought the Coleman "Air-O-Lamp," followed soon after by the Coleman "Quick-Lite." These early lamps and lanterns were imprinted with the "Sunshine Safety" name. Over the years Coleman continued to sell pressurized-fuel products to this company, although Sunshine probably purchased pressurized-fuel stoves, irons, lamps and lanterns from sources other than Coleman. By 1926, three members of Coleman's management were serving on Sunshine's board of directors. In 1928, the Sunshine Safety Company merged with Coleman Lamp Company and ceased to operate as a separate company.

Advertisement for Sunshine Safety Lantern.

Sunshine Safety Lantern

This model was manufactured by Coleman as the model "AL", 1915 – 1916.
Coleman also sold the model "L" Arc Lantern to this company, but they may have purchased lanterns from other companies as well. Probably marked "Sunshine Safety".

Very rare.

Mantle Lamp Company

Although more famous for its Aladdin table lamps, the Mantle Lamp Company, at 223 West Jackson Boulevard, Chicago, also manufactured two styles of pressurized-fuel lanterns using gasoline, and a combination pressurized-fuel lantern using either gasoline or kerosene. These were marked "Aladdin."

Advertisement for the Model A lantern.

During the Second World War, Mantle Lamp contracted with the United States military to manufacture a pressurized-fuel lantern using gasoline. This was designated model "A." Information available indicates that these pressurized-fuel lanterns were not sold to the general public until after 1946. That year, production was started with the model "PL-1" (Pressure Lantern-1). Sold in the United States and overseas, this model continued to be manufactured for fourteen more years. During this time there was a very short-lived model 310, manufactured for sale in Great Britain. Mantle Lamp Company ceased operations in 1960.

A
1940 – 1946

Manufactured for the United States armed services. Unknown quantities, if any, were sold to the general public after 1946.

Apparently the tools used to manufacture this lantern were the property of the United States government and were returned to the Army in 1946.

Rare.

310
1958 – 1959

Finish: chrome, or green enamel.

Sold overseas, mainly in Great Britain.

Very rare.

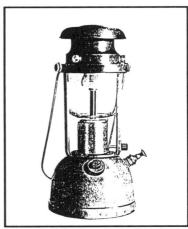

PL-1
1946 – 1960

Dual-fuel lantern.

Had a slide lever marked "Kero" or "Gas," to be placed in position depending on fuel used. Kerosene was recommended, but if not available, then gasoline could be used.

Rare: in the United States.

Common: in Europe.

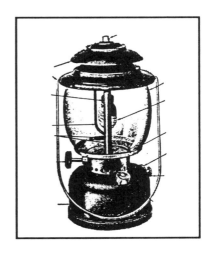

Coleman Quick-Lite

REGISTERED TRADE MARK—U. S. PATENT OFFICE

Lamps and Lanterns

"The Sunshine
of the Night"

"The Light of a
Thousand Uses"

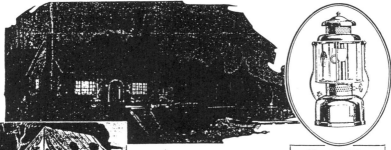

The Quick-Lite Lantern
Just the Thing

For Camping—for your tent, your cabin in the woods or mountains, your cottage on the lake, your vacation home.

For Hunting Trips of all kinds—a regular day-light maker for sportsmen everywhere—in the everglades of Florida, the coon woods of Arkansas, or the big game wilds of the Rockies.

For Night Fishing and boating—on the docks, in the boat house, the launch, the canoe, the "18-footer", the yacht, the "steamer."

For Porch Parties, picnics, lawn socials and "night out" stunts of all kinds—carnivals, street fairs, tent shows, concessions, public meetings.

For Auto Touring
—"pitching camp is easy" (see story on other side of this sheet.)

For Any Job of work, any night, any where, any weather—teaming, plowing, harvesting, ditching, feeding, grinding, choring. The handy light for mills, elevators, factories, warehouses, night watchmen, plumbers — contractors—everybody.

Here's Why You'll Like It

300 Candle Power of pure-white, brilliant light. Brighter than 20 old style oil lanterns.

Lights with matches. Makes and burns its own gas from common motor gasoline.

No greasy wicks to trim; no dirty chimney to wash; no smoke; no soot; no odor.

Can't spill fuel or explode—even if tipped over. Can't be filled while lighted.

Give more than 40 hours brilliant service per gallon of fuel.

Cost to use less than 15 cents a week.

Built of Brass, heavily nickeled. Inspected, tested, guaranteed.

Has mica globe with metal reflector. Is wind-proof, rain-proof and bug-proof. Keeps right on shining in the wildest weather.

Circa 1921 flyer for Coleman Quick-Lite lantern.

Hydro-Carbon Light Company
Coleman Lamp Company
Coleman Company, Inc.

William Coffin Coleman was born in Chatham, a small village in Columbia County, upstate New York, on May 5, 1870. He died in 1957. The house he was born in no longer exists, and a supermarket sits on the site. The road is still called Coleman Avenue after his father, Robert Coleman.

During the early part of 1871, Coleman's parents made the 1,500-mile journey, by train and covered wagon, to Labette County, Kansas. Here his family operated a small farm and soon attained good standing in the community. During Coleman's eleventh year his father died. His increased responsibility on the farm seriously slowed his daylight schooling studies, and poor eyesight prevented night studies. Determined that Coleman would have a good education, his mother leased the farm and moved them to Parsons, Kansas, when he was fifteen. At nineteen he entered the State Teachers College at Emporia, where he completed a four-year course in three years.

Upon graduating he taught a year at Ottawa University in Kansas and studied languages in his spare time. He then became principal of schools at Blue Rapids, Kansas. After two years there he gave up teaching to study law at Kansas University. To finance his tuition he sold sewing machines for two years, dividing his time between selling and studying. He later said the fact he was forced to be a salesman and to succeed in his work was perhaps the greatest blessing of his early years.

In the winter of 1899, W. C. Coleman was working in
Blockton, Alabama, selling typewriters. Blockton was like so many
other small communities, with boardwalks and dirt streets. When
evening came, Coleman left his hotel to visit prospective buyers of
these "marvelous" new typewriters. His day vision was poor and his
night vision was even worse, but as he stepped out of the hotel that
night, he saw what was to become the start of his lighting business.
Across the street in a drug store window, shining brighter than any
light he had ever seen, was an amazingly bright lamp. Inside the
store, he discovered he could read the labels on the medicine
bottles from this light. Upon closer inspection Coleman noted that
the lamp was burning pressurized gasoline and instead of a wick it
had a mantle.

Hydro-Carbon offices and factory on Wichita's North Main Street. About 1905.

The store owner could not tell him anything about the lamp. It
had been left by a drummer (as in to "drum up" trade), a salesmen
who would leave an item in a store window and come back a few
days later to see if there were any orders or interest. The next
morning the lamp was gone.

For weeks Coleman thought about how nice it would be to own
such a lamp so he could read at night. When he came across the
lamp again, he this time spoke to the salesman, who informed him
that it was an "Efficient" lamp, manufactured by Edward Miller and
Sons of Connecticut, for the patent holder, a Mr. Irby, of
Irby-Gilliland, crockery wholesalers in Memphis, Tennessee. Not
long after this encounter, Irby-Gilliland was named in a lawsuit

brought by salesmen who had bought territories from them, but were not able to sell the lamps. The firm decided it would hire a good salesman to prove the product could be sold. The job was offered to Coleman.

With a stock of sixteen lamps he set off to sell in Kingfisher, Oklahoma Territory. He selected Kingfisher because it was a relatively well-populated frontier area with no electricity. He could get no one to buy them, however, and learned that about a year earlier a salesman had sold similar lamps and within a month they were out of order. No one had faith in them.

To counteract this Coleman hit upon the idea of selling a lighting service rather than the lamps themselves. Calling his new rental company the Hydro-Carbon Light Company, he offered the lamps for rent at a dollar per week. Part of his rental agreement stated that if the light failed within each weekly rental there would be no fee. This was a "no-lose" situation for the renter and soon Coleman had more than 100 rental contracts. As he only had sixteen lamps, he went back to Labette County and asked his brother-in-law to loan him $1,000. With the money he bought 100 more Efficient lamps, returned to Kingfisher and started the rentals. By 1900 Coleman had rental stores in seventeen locations.

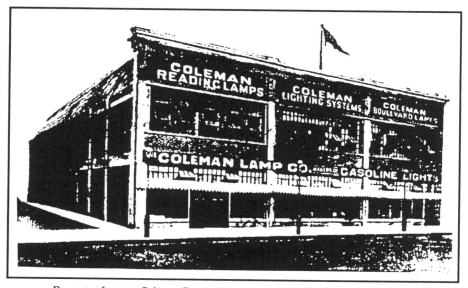

First unit of present Coleman Factory A as it was in 1913. The building also housed the firm's offices and research laboratory.

In 1901 Irby-Gilliland offered to sell their business to him for $3,000, allowing him to pay it off at a monthly rate of $250. The deal included the patent for the Efficient lamp. Less than a month later Coleman opened his sales headquarters in Wichita, Kansas, at 128 East Second Street, and was soon established.

In 1903, Coleman moved to 311 North Main Street. Over the next two years additions were built on this building to accommodate the growing business. During this time, the Efficient lamp being manufactured for him by Edward Miller Company was renamed the "Coleman." The first of these lamps arrived in Wichita in 1903.

That same year the renting of lamps was phased out of Coleman's business, leaving a large number of lamps that needed to be reconditioned and sold. The testing, reconditioning and sale of these lamps was the beginning of the evolution of the Hydro-Carbon Light Company into the Coleman Lamp Company, for in 1904 Coleman decided to start manufacturing these lamps and lighting systems himself.

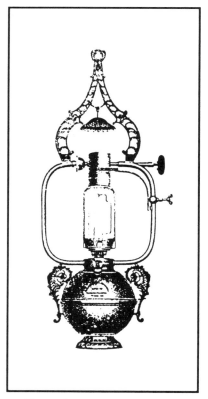

The Arc Lamp was the first gasoline pressure lamp to bear the Coleman name. Originally it was called the "Efficient Lamp."

The year 1909 saw the Hydro-Carbon Company incorporated, and the erection of a two-story, 75' X 144' building at 212 North St. Francis Street in Wichita. After two years of experimenting, Coleman was finally satisfied with the new lamp design, which was an improvement on the Efficient lamp. He patented it as the Coleman model "R" (for "Reading") lamp. In August, 1909, the first 120 "R" lamps came off the production line.

A tent in Las Vegas, Nevada, was the home of an early day Hydro-Carbon Company branch operation, circa 1911.

Sometime in 1910 Coleman produced a small pressurized-fuel gasoline hot plate. These proved popular, and in 1911 a corner of the Coleman factory was set aside to manufacture these hot plates. Coleman also contracted with the National Stove Company of Lorain, Ohio to manufacture for him several models of stoves and ranges to be sold under the trade name "Insurance." This line also included ovens, water heaters and utility burners. By 1921 the Coleman Company was manufacturing all its own stoves. All were pressurized-fuel using gasoline. In 1913 the company changed its name from the Hydro-Carbon Light Company to the Coleman Lamp Company.

At this time the only portable outdoor lanterns available from manufacturers were wick-burning kerosene lanterns. While very poor in light output, they had one tremendous advantage over the brighter indoor pressurized-fuel gasoline lamps, as they could be moved anywhere, any time, in- or out-of-doors. The need for an outdoor pressurized-fuel lantern using gasoline was noted by Coleman, and his design team produced many prototypes over the next few years. The lantern had to be sturdy, withstand rough usage, and not leak if held upside down. The design they finally settled on was an adaptation of a gasoline

Advertisement for Quick-Lite, July, 1926.

pressurized-fuel Coleman System hollow-wire light which had earlier been designed as an outdoor street lamp. These were lamps on poles, with no individual fonts. Fuel was delivered to each lamp via hollow wire from a central fuel container.

The new design reduced its size and added a fuel font and bail, so the lamp now was portable — it could be carried, or hung on a post. After many experimental models, the final one was placed into production. It was called the "Arc" lantern. The first of these portable pressurized-fuel lanterns using gasoline were produced by Coleman in 1914, designed for farm, market, emergency and rescue

Just Like Having a Gas Well in Your Own Back Yard

As gas and electric service spread throughout the land, farm and suburban families beyond their reach turned to gasoline as a means of release from the inconveniences of wood and coal for heating, cooking, ironing, and lighting. A page from a Coleman circular of the 1920s suggested that using Coleman products was like having a gas well in the back yard.

use, where bright light was needed and electricity was not available.

The year 1914 saw Coleman purchase his Wichita business rival, Incandescent Light & Supply Company. This merger gave Coleman facilities for manufacturing the inverted rag mantles so essential in producing the brilliant white pressurized-fuel light. That same year Coleman also purchased the Yale Light Company, of Chicago. By the end of the First World War the Coleman factory had grown substantially. From 1914 on Coleman products diversified into many different areas, but all were connected in some way to his original gasoline pressurized-fuel lamp.

By the end of the Second World War, more homes worldwide were heated by Coleman heaters than any other make of heater. Today many Coleman products are used in this and other countries for camping. Their camp stoves, small heaters, lanterns, lamps, clothing irons, cookers, water heaters, radiant heaters and other products are found in homes around the world, particularly in Third World countries. The demand for lanterns and portable stoves continues to grow; they are the main products of what is now called the Coleman Company, Incorporated.

Variations in Coleman Model Numbers

The difference between models of the same type or in the same "series" (e.g., 200 and 200A), is not always easy to discern. There usually is no way of telling them apart, for the added letter(s) typically only signalled some small design change, or minor parts materials change, or a subassembly put together differently on the production line. Even the introduction of a new parts supply vendor might have been cause for the addition of a letter after the number. For example, with the 200 and 200A, the latter was added simply because of different finishes on the fonts.

In the Coleman factory, did the same model numbers run concurrently (e.g., 200, 200A, etc.)? The answer is yes, as far as records indicate. The dates of manufacture which are listed with each lantern in this book are taken from the shipping ledgers, not from the production records. This is because the shipping records are almost complete, while early production records were not maintained. Therefore, the first date listed here for each lantern was taken from the first time that model appears in the shipping records, and the last date from when the last date shipped is recorded.

The volume of business for Coleman was so large that it was rare to manufacture for stock. Orders were filled from the production line. For this reason the shipping dates will quite accurately reflect production dates. Coleman lanterns are marked "Coleman" on the font or globe rest, along with the model number for most. Some are also marked with numbers for date and month, or vice versa.

"L" Arc Lantern
1914 – 1918

Candlepower: 300
Height: 20"; weight: 12 lbs, less fuel.
Fuel: gasoline.
Font: one gallon; 8" diameter.
Mantles: two; inverted rag type.
Chimney: glass; diameter, 12"; height, 10 1/4".
Torch lighting.
Finish: nickel-plated ventilator; brass, nickel-plated font; some fonts, zinc-coated steel.
Accessories: air pump, lighting torch and wrench. No model number or production dates were stamped on this model.

A heavy-duty lantern for use on farms, docks, construction sites and for other outdoor work. Also used to light camp meetings, tent shows, and as standby lighting during power interruptions. This model was also manufactured for the Sunshine Safety Lamp Company from 1915 to 1917. It is not known if they were marked "Coleman" or "Sunshine Safety Company," or if they were marked at all.

This is a sectional view of the L lantern, showing the position of the mantles, combination filler plug and air valve and ventilator. The cone-shaped metal hood was to protect mantles from the wind.

Very rare.

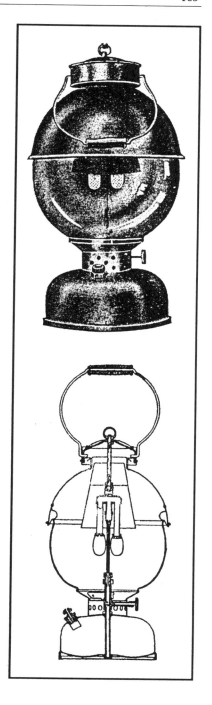

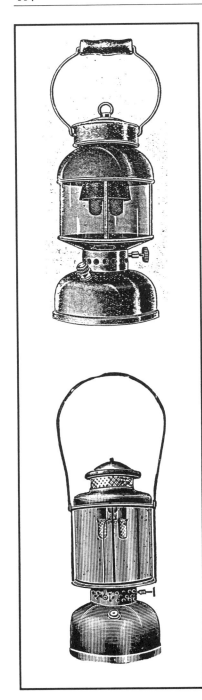

AL, IL and NL Air-O-Lanterns
1915 – 1916

AL

Candlepower: 300.
Height: 16"; weight: 9 lbs, less fuel.
Fuel: gasoline. Font: 3 pints; 7" diameter.
Mantles: two.
Chimney: mica; 6" diameter; 4 1/2" high.
Torch lighting.
Finish: ventilator, brass, nickel plated; font,
brass; some fonts, lead-coated steel.

No model number or production dates
were stamped on this model. A strong
dependable lantern; smaller and lighter
weight than the L Arc. The lead-coated
steel looks duller than the zinc coated.

IL

Height: 14". Font: smaller than the AL.
Chimney: mica; 5" diameter; 5" high.
Generator equipped with automatic tip
(pinhole) cleaner.

The size and shape of the IL lantern
would set the style for Coleman two-
mantle gasoline- and kerosene-pressure
lanterns for more than 70 years.

NL. Same specification as the IL, but
with a plain generator tip. No model
numbers or production dates were
stamped on these models.

Both the AL and the IL were
manufactured by Coleman for the
Sunshine Safety Lamp Company, and
the Yale Light Company under their
respective names. A variation of the IL
lantern was made for Sears, Roebuck
during this same period.

Very rare: all models.

LQ327 Quick-Lite Lantern.
1917 – 1930

Candlepower: 300.
Fuel: gasoline.
Font: 3 pints; 6" diameter.
Mantles: two; inverted rag type.
Chimney: mica; with match access door.
Match lighting.
Finish: nickel-plated brass font; ventilator, nickel plated.

Patented loop generator; combination filler plug and air valve; separate air pump. Symmetrical air holes in chimney base and ventilator. Shipped with pump-cleaning pick, wrench and spare Q99 generator.

This was the first of the match lighting Coleman lanterns. Access for lighting was through a small door in the chimney. The chimney was made of mica and constructed from thirteen pieces assembled together on a frame, 5 3/8" high x 4 7/8" diameter, with a sliding-access door.

Two styles of generators can be found on these models: the Q99 coil and the Q77 straight generator.

LQ 327 lanterns manufactured between 1917 and 1923 have no numbers indicating month and year produced. Also called the QL **(Quick Light).**

Very rare.

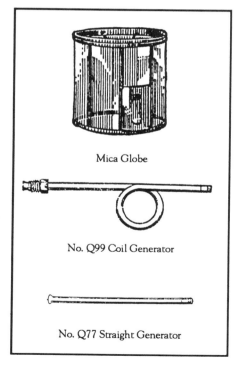

Mica Globe

No. Q99 Coil Generator

No. Q77 Straight Generator

THE SUNSHINE OF THE NIGHT

Stamped Logo Design

R55 Jumbo Rotary Generator

LQ427 Quick Lite Lantern
1920 – 1930

Candlepower: 300.
Fuel: gasoline.
Font: 3 pints.
Chimney: mica; with match lighting access door.
Match lighting.
Finish: ventilator, green vitreous enamel; nickel-plated brass font.
Generator: choice of Q99 loop or straight Q77.

Distinctive features are vitreous enamel ventilator, built-in pump and "Coleman Quick Lite" in perforated lettering in the chimney base rest. Lanterns manufactured between 1924 and 1930 can be identified by a metal stamping on the font bearing the words "Coleman – The Sunshine of the Night" and a sunburst design. Beneath this design will be found numerals which indicate the year and month of manufacture. For example: "511" stood for the year (1925) and the month (November). Lanterns made before 1924 do not have date information.

The R55 generator can be found on some Quick Lite lanterns. This was not standard but rather, indicates that a previous owner has updated his lantern with the larger self-cleaning type used on Coleman Instant-Lite models. Lanterns returned to the factory for repair will also have the R55 generator.

Rare.

E20
1925 – 1929

Variation of the LQ327, with a larger, 4-quart steel font, and a steel wool dust screen to prevent dust from clogging the burner air tubes. One filling was said to give 60 hours of brilliant service.

Approximately 10,000 were manufactured, including some early models with a 5-quart font and a pressure gauge.

Used to lengthen the light hours during winter, causing chickens to lay more eggs. Also called the **Poultry House** lantern.

Very rare.

200 and 200A
1950 – 1983

Height: 12 3/16"; weight: 4 lbs.
Fuel: gasoline.
Font: 1 3/5 pints; 5 1/8" diameter.
Single mantle.
Globe: Pyrex glass globe.
Instant lighting.
Finish: **200:** *font, bright nickel; ventilator, bright red enamel.* **200A:** *font and ventilator, bright red enamel.*
Except: in 1950, both models had a heavy bright nickel font; 1981 – 1983 ventilator and font of both models were painted green.

Designed with a built-in pump and improved T66 generator. Estimated production was well over five million.

Common.

No. T66 (Roto-Type) Generator

202
1954 – 1964

Fuel: gasoline.
Single mantle.
Instant lighting.
Finish: ventilator, green porcelain enamel; font, brass, extra nickel plated; all other exposed parts, cadmium plated.

Close in style to the 200A but designed to be highly resistant to corrosion. Date stamping is month and year (e.g., "116" is November, 1956.

Common to all single-mantle lanterns 200, 202, and 220A models was the T66 roto-type generator. A small hook at one end engaged a cleaning needle operated by a rotary lever built into the lantern burner. The T66 could also be used on the 234, 242, and 243 models.

Rare.

220 and 220B
1927 – 1941

Fuel: gasoline.
Font: 2 pints.
Chimney: 1927 – 1929 the 220 model had mica chimney with lighter-access door. Later models had Pyrex heat-resistant globes.
Finish: brass, nickel plated font; ventilator, green vitreous enamel.

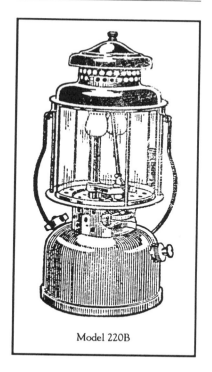

Model 220B

After 1928 the 220 had its generator parallel to the air tube.
1930 – 1941, the 220B had roto-type generator set at an angle to the air tube (shown).

Font had one-piece filler plug, built-in air pump, and imprinted sunburst design.

Prior to 1930 the date on these models was stamped month/year; after this date it was stamped year/month.

No model 220As were produced.

An undetermined quantity of the 220 and 220B were sold to the Atchison, Topeka and Santa Fe Railroad for emergency lighting. Many of these lanterns were still being returned to the Coleman factory for servicing as late as the early 1950s.

During World War II there was a limited production of model 220; whom these were manufactured for is not known.

Common.

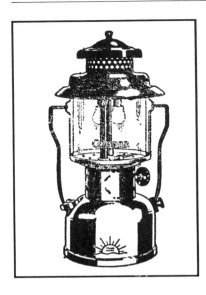

220C, 220D and 220E
1945 – 1963

Fuel: gasoline.
Font: 2 pints; 6" diameter.
Mantles: two; inverted.
Globe: Pyrex heat resistant; straight sided.
Instant lighting.
Finish: font, green vitreous enamel.
Globe rest was aluminum, with dot/dash-pattern air holes; space on this rest used for stamping month and year manufactured.
Generator, rotary type with built-in cleaning needle, type T44G.
All models had fonts with built-in pump and hand-operated filler plug.

A few of these models had month/year of manufacture stamped under the font. The 220 series made in 1951 and subsequent years, had copper-brazed steel fonts.

The postwar 220C was redesigned from the pre-war 220B model.

Common.

220F – H, 220J, K
1964 – 1983

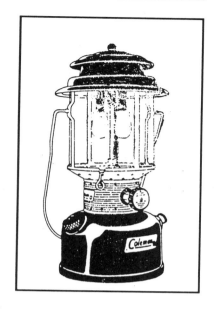

Fuel: gasoline.
Font: two pints; 6" diameter.
Mantles: two; inverted.
Globe: Pyrex heat resistant; straight sided.
Instant lighting.
Finish: brass font; ventilator and font, green vitreous enamel.
Generator, T44G rotary type with built-in cleaning needle.

Their specifications were the same as the 220C, but in 1964 the 220F was re-styled to give it a slightly lower profile. All dimensions but the overall height remained the same. New height was 13 7/8". Included in the new look was an aluminum globe rest, or collar, that had a ribbed surface and circular air holes. The month/year of manufacture were stamped in a space on the collar.

Common.

228 and 228B
1927 – 1941

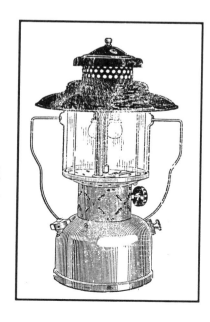

Fuel: gasoline.
Globe: Pyrex heat resistant, straight sided; globe rest had dot/dash air-hole design.
Instant lighting.
Finish: ventilator, green vitreous enamel; white vitreous enamel on the underside.

This 228 series design is easily recognized by the wide 8 3/4" ventilator. Month and year manufactured were stamped in a space on the collar.

No model 228A was produced. In 1945 the 228B was reintroduced as the 228C.

Rare.

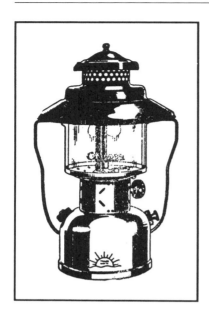

228C, 228D and 228E
1945 – 1963

Fuel: gasoline.
Instant lighting.
Finish: font, brass.

Apart from the bail support location, the postwar models of the 228 wide-ventilator lanterns underwent few changes from pre-war models.

The size, finish, and capacity of the font were unchanged, as was the lantern's generator with built-in tip cleaner. Also unchanged was the dot/dash air-hole design on the globe rest, and the location of date and year produced.

A major production change on these models occurred in 1952 when the brass font was replaced with copper-brazed steel. This material was then used for these models until production ended in 1963.

Common.

228F – 228J
1963 – 1979

Features are the same as the 220C, 220D and 220E, but in 1964 the lantern's ventilator was re-styled to achieve a more streamlined appearance. Changes also were made to the globe rest. The new overall height of 13 7/8" and the ribbed globe rest further enhanced the appearance of lanterns made between 1964 and 1979.

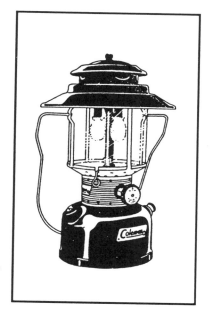

The ribbed globe rest was the same pattern as that established for the 220F lantern. The 228 series lanterns were replaced by the 228 Gold Standard model, which looked the same as the 228 but was marked "Gold Standard". Production of 228 series lanterns ended in 1979.

No Coleman lanterns with this 8 3/4" ventilator were manufactured after 1979.

Rare.

221, 222, 223, 225, 227
1928 – 1939

Coleman was committed to the production of gasoline-fueled pressure lanterns from 1914 on. However, in 1928 and 1929 they also began production of the 222 and 223 kerosene burning models. These were assigned to the Coleman Export Division in Chicago. In 1930, production of the 222 and the 223 and other models that would follow (221, 225, 227) were assigned to the Coleman factory in Toronto. No drawings or specimens of these models are known to exist.

This model 222 is not to be confused with the Col-Max model 222.

Very rare.

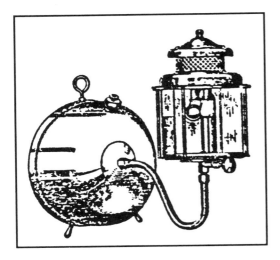

B327 or CQ
Circa 1920

Font: nickel-plated brass.
Chimney: mica.

This was an unusual style: a combination of a standard LQ327 outdoor lantern with the font, control valve and fuel tube of an indoor BQ bracket lamp.

Can be found marked "CQ" on the base and "Coleman, made in Canada."

Very rare.

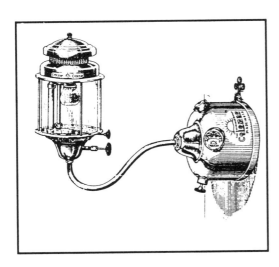

124B
Circa 1930

Fuel: kerosene, gasoline, benzene, benzol or paraffin.
Globe: Pyrex heat resistant glass.
Finish: brass, nickel plated.
Automatic tip cleaner; built-in pump and pressure gauge.

These are unlikely to be found in the United States, as they were made for export and sold overseas.

Very rare.

242
1932 – 1935

Height: 11 1/2"; weight: 4 lbs.
Fuel: gasoline.
Single mantle.
Globe: Pyrex heat resistant, straight sided.
Instant lighting.
*Finish: ventilator top, green vitreous
enamel, 4 3/4" diameter; font, brass,
nickel plated.*

The 242 was first in a series of single-
mantle, instant lighting gasoline
lanterns.

Rare.

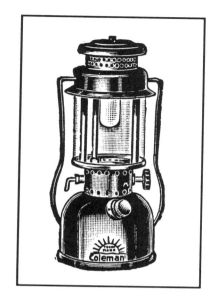

242A
1935 – 1936

Instant lighting.

Similar in shape, size and finish to model
242, but with a Pyrex bulge-style globe.

Other 242 series lanterns:
242B:
1937 – 1941.
242C:
1945 – 1950.

Instant lighting.

Style and design similar to the 242A.
All models equipped with instant
lighting feature and a font with a
built-in pump.

Production of 242B was interrupted
in 1941 by United States entry into
World War II.

Rare: all models.

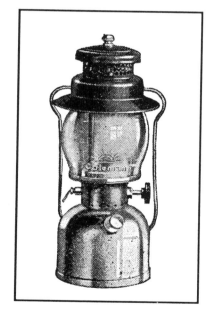

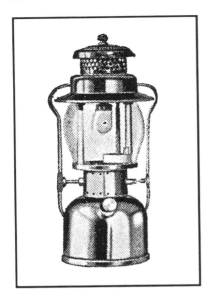

242K
1935 – 1938

Fuel: kerosene.
Single mantle.
Globe: Pyrex heat resistant; bulge style.
Finish: aluminum ventilator; font, brass,
nickel plated; after 1936, enameled.

Vertical mounted generator, with large
pre-heater cup attached to the generator
base. Font had built-in pressure pump.
Manufactured in Toronto, Canada.

Rare.

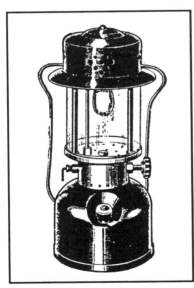

243
1936 – 1937

Candlepower: 175.
Height: 11 1/2"; weight: 3 lbs.
Fuel: gasoline.
Font: 1 1/3 pints; 5" diameter.
Chimney: mica, straight sided.
Instant lighting.
Finish: font, brass, blue lacquer;
ventilator, blue lacquer.

Operated between 7 and 9 hours on a full
font. Model 243 was developed and
manufactured in the Depression years to
fill a perceived need for a lower-priced
lantern. Resistant to strong wind and
rain, it retailed in 1936 for $4.45.

Very rare.

Col-Max Kerosene Lanterns
222, 333, and 555
1939 – 1970

A distinguishing feature of all Col-Max lanterns was their chrome-nickel finish and bright red ventilator tops. They had a single mantle, and a preheater cup attached to the generator.

Shown are two models, one with ventilator modified to throw light downward.

222: 200 candlepower.
333: 300 candlepower.
555: 500 candlepower.

A limited number of the 222 and 333 were manufactured 1939 – 1941 in the United States, specifically for export to countries where the European style "Petromax" lantern from Germany was well established. After 1941 production was shifted to the Toronto, Canada factory. From 1955 to 1970 production was moved to Hong Kong. During this time a model 555 was also manufactured there. However, from 1955 until 1975 there was no mention of kerosene lanterns in the Coleman sales or service literature for their United States dealers.

The European-style Col-Max lantern was especially targeted toward operators of bazaar stalls in the Orient and commercial fishers in the South Pacific. Iran also was a prime market for this type of outdoor lighting.

All models made after 1946 were equipped with a pressure gauge and shipped with a brass filling can, filter funnel, wrench, needle key, mantle, pump seal, gas tip and needle. Some models also had a "Rapid Light" attachment to expedite the lighting procedure.

Very rare.

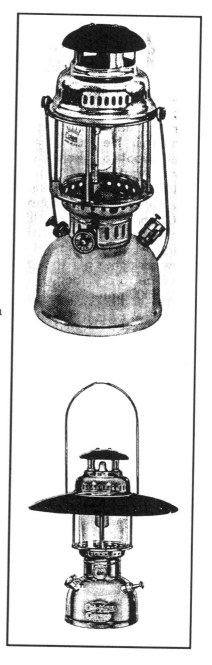

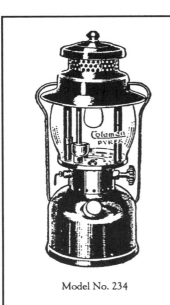

Model No. 234

Model No. 235

234, 235, and 236
1935 – 1940

Height: 235 and 236 were 14 1/2"; the 234 was slightly smaller.
Fuel: kerosene.
Font: 2 pints; built-in pump.
Mantle: two on the 235; one on the 234.
Finish: font and ventilator, light green enamel over steel.
Burning time 10 – 12 hours.

The generator tube had a large preheater fuel cup attached. Both the 234 and 235 models were manufactured in the Wichita, Kansas factory from 1935 – 1940.

Common to both models was a decal with the word "Kerosene" and the model number on the front of the font.

Company records indicate the 234 and 235 were targeted for the coastal areas of the United States and Canada rather than overseas. Domestic production on both these models ended due to the increase in military orders. During World War II there was a limited production of a model 236; whom these were for is a mystery.

Very rare.

237, 237A and 249
1939 – 1974

Number 237: 1939 – 1941
Number 237A: 1946 – 1974
Number 249: 1949 – 1961
Candlepower: 500.
Height: 14 1/2"; weight: 6 lbs.
Fuel: kerosene or gasoline.
Font: 2 pints.
Single mantle.
Globe: Pyrex heat resistant; bulge style; diameter 5 1/4".
Finish: ventilator, steel with green porcelain enamel; font, brass, nickel plated.
Primer cup attached to self-cleaning generator. Font had built-in air pump.

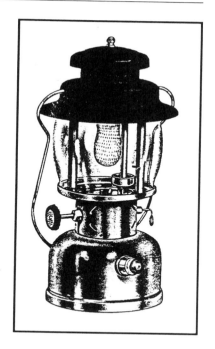

First production in 1939 by Coleman Lamp and Stove Co., Ltd.; none manufactured during World War II. Production resumed in 1946 (as 237A) at the Toronto, Canada factory, and at the same time an unknown number of Model 237A were manufactured, under license agreement, by U.S. Carbon and Carbide at Sao Paulo, Brazil.

The 237 and 237A were mainly distributed in Central America and the Caribbean, with limited distribution in the United States and Canada.

A limited quantity of Model 249 was manufactured from 1949 – 1961. These were a down-sized version of the 237.

Rare: all three models.

252 and 252A
1942 – 1945

These military lanterns were designed and developed in 1942 through the joint efforts of engineers representing: U.S. Quartermaster Corps; Aladdin Lamp Company; American Gas Machine Company; Prentiss-Waber Company (later Preway, Inc.); Coleman Company.

The lanterns resulting from the combined efforts of the design committee followed the general outline of the Coleman No. 220B pressurized-fuel lantern, but with a major change in the lantern generator and burner.

Other variations from the Coleman 220 domestic lantern were its single mantle and army olive drab enamel, with two yellow decals one listing directions for lighting and servicing, the other stating "fill with any type of gasoline."

Included was a small funnel to aid in fueling, fastened with a short chain to the lantern. A compartment was built into the font to store a spare generator and mantles.

The greatest percentage of these lanterns were manufactured by Coleman, but to determine the year and name of manufacturer, examine the underside of the font.

Coleman entered into production of both models in late 1942, and by 1945 approximately one million military lanterns had been manufactured and shipped to the U.S. and allied forces.

Rare.

5101
1955 – 1963

Height: 13 1/8"; weight: 2 1/2 lbs.
Fuel: butane gas.
Globe: heat resistant glass.
Finish: font and ventilator, steel with green enamel.

A wire cage surrounded the fuel container, providing stability. Ease of lighting, lighter weight, and resistance to wind and rain made this lantern a favorite for use on patio, picnics and other summertime activities.

Introduced in 1955, this was the first of a long line of Coleman lanterns to make use of the special properties of liquid petroleum. The fuel required no pressurization and was easily lighted when outside temperatures were above 38 degrees F. A disposable container of fuel would last up to 4 hours.

Common.

5120 and 5122
1963 – 1969

A redesign of the earlier model 5101, with a new base to facilitate easier installation and removal of the butane container. It also gave the lantern greater stability. The globe, valve, generator, ventilator and bail remained the same. Light characteristics were similar to the earlier 5101. Finish of ventilator and base was green enamel.

The model 5122 was the same as the 5120 but included a pressure gauge. Shown is the 5120.

Common.

5107, 5114, 5151A and 5152A
1973 – present

5107, 5114
1973 – 1985

5151A, 5152A
1985 – Present

Height: 16 1/2"; base, 7 3/4" diameter.
Fuel: propane.
Mantle: one on models 5107 and 5151A; two on models 5114 and 5152A.
Globe: heat resistant clear glass.
Finish: ventilator, green porcelain enamel with matching base holding the propane bottle.
Regulators were built into the lamp base to maintain constant pressure at 15 psi.

A steady increase in the use of propane for lighting, heating and cooking brought a shift in consumer demand for this more versatile fuel. The transition from butane to propane occurred over several years, but by 1973 Coleman had a single-mantle lantern, with a 14.1 ounce or 16.4 ounce propane bottle. Propane lanterns could also be attached to larger, refillable bottles when an adapter and regulator were used.

Common.

201-700
1977 – 1980

Height: 11 5/8"; weight: 4 lbs.
Fuel: kerosene.
Font: 1 3/8 pints; 5 1/8" diameter.
Single mantle.

Beginning in 1977 this kerosene-pressure lantern was manufactured and sold in the United States. While this model appeared in catalogues, for some reason it was not extensively promoted.

Rare.

214A700
1980 – 1993

Kerosene lanterns made after 1980 were similar to the 201-700 single-mantle lantern, but were marked "214A700", and had a different globe.

Common.

639B700
1993 to present

Height: 13 1/2"; base, 6" diameter.
Fuel: kerosene.
Font: 2 pints.
Burning time on high, approximately 5 1/2 hours.

In 1993 Coleman added to its line this kerosene-pressure lantern, said to have 50% greater light output than the smaller 214A700.

Common.

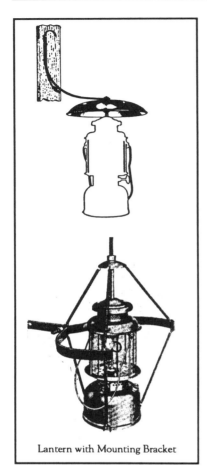

Lantern with Mounting Bracket

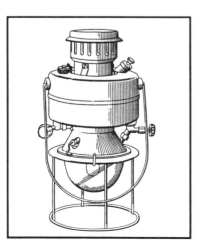

204

A wall hanger for lanterns.
Shield: 11" diameter; 2" high.
Finish: green enamel.

Iron hanger had slots for hanging onto nails or screws. Advertised for use in barns, poultry houses, dairies, garages. Retail price during 1937 was $1.95.

Rare.

480
1914 – 1920

Special bracket (left) to mount a lantern on a vehicle. With it, the lantern was suspended on springs to reduce jarring and shaking.

Used on farm tractors for night plowing, or night-time hauling on motor vehicles.

Rare.

Upside Down Lantern

Fuel: leaded or regular gasoline.

Designed primarily for the U.S. Army, for use in field hospitals, and for map reading beyond the reach of electric service. The design of this lantern was such that no shadows were thrown, as the light was underneath.

Filed as Patent No. 173,397, issued November 2, 1954, for its "ornamental design."

It would be rare indeed to come across one of these as Coleman only manufactured approximately 50 in the late 1950s.

Very rare.

Prentiss-Waber Product Company

Prentiss-Waber was operating by 1915 in Grand Rapids (in 1920 to become Wisconsin Rapids), Wisconsin. A catalogue of their products between 1926 and 1936 shows they manufactured gasoline pressurized-fuel lanterns, stoves and hot plates. During World War II they cooperated with Coleman Company and American Gas Company in the design of a pressurized-fuel gasoline lantern for the armed services. In conjunction with other manufacturers they produced lanterns and possibly other pressurized-fuel appliances for the military. After 1952 they changed their name to Preway,, Inc. They went out of business late in the 1980s. Their lanterns were marked "Prentiss-Waber."

Yale Light Company

Yale Light Company of Chicago was a distributor of pressurized-fuel lighting systems. Its main sales products were pressurized-fuel gasoline and kerosene table lamps and outdoor lanterns. Pressurized-fuel stoves, burners and irons were among other items included in their sales product line. Two of their table lamps were made by the American Gas Machine Company, and it is not known if other Chicago manufacturers produced lamps for them. Coleman was the sole manufacturer of the pressurized-fuel gasoline lanterns that Yale sold. Yale remained a good customer of Coleman products until it was merged in October, 1914 with the Wichita-based Coleman Company. At this time Yale went out of business, but its product catalogue was revised by Coleman and mailed to customers for another two to three years under the Yale name. These catalogues are recognizable by the over-stamping of the Coleman name and address. Trademarks found on Yale lanterns are "Yale" and "Arco-lite." Most of Yale's products were sold in Chicago, northern Illinois, and southern Wisconsin.

No. 100
1915 – 1916

Candlepower: 400.

This was the Coleman AL, but marked "Yale." Packaged with one spare mantle, globe lighter, extra generator and instruction manual.

Very rare.

No. 111
1915 – 1916

This was the Coleman IL, but marked "Yale."

Advertised as smaller and lighter than the 100, therefore easier to carry. The design is such that the light is "thrown out and higher" more than other styles.

Very rare.

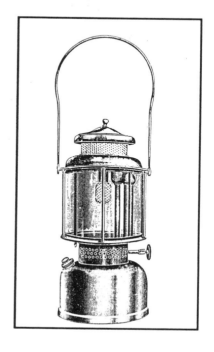

Montgomery Ward & Company

Beginning in 1872, with a capital investment of $2,400, Aaron Montgomery Ward and his partner George R. Thorpe operated a mail order company out of a loft over a stable on Kinsie Street in Chicago. During the early stages of the company, they concentrated on selling to the farmers of Illinois and Iowa. From the beginning they followed a policy of allowing customers to return goods they found unsatisfactory. In 1872 their first catalogue was eight pages. By 1876 it had 150 pages and many illustrations. During 1888 annual sales reached one million dollars.

Many different types and styles of lanterns were sold by Montgomery Ward over the years. Their lantern manufacturing sources included R. E. Dietz Company, American Gas Machine Company, Coleman Lamp Company and Akron Lamp Company. The dead-flame, hot-blast and cold-blast lanterns they offered were mainly manufactured by Dietz. Some of these can be found marked "Wards." One trade name used by Montgomery Ward on pressurized-fuel lanterns was "Nulite." These Nulite lanterns were sold in the 1930s and are believed to have been manufactured by Chicago Solar Light Company.

Identifying and Pricing Lanterns

The illustrations in this book and my earlier volume are intended to help you develop a sense of which lanterns are common and which are rare. Study them until you are familiar with the different types and styles, and their periods. Once you have this general concept, factor in an awareness of what "streamline style" dead flame, hot-blast and cold-blast lanterns look like. They can resemble their 19th-century counterparts, but their crimp marks, from the newer manufacturing process, betray their post 1920s origins. The parts of older tubular lanterns were soldered together; the parts of the "streamlined" lanterns of the 1930s and after were crimped and overlapped by machine.

Pre-1900 marine lanterns were usually made of copper or brass, and can be distinguished by their ornate hinges, handles, etc. Most have glass globes. A few of these early marine lanterns were manufactured with Fresnel lenses, but these are very rare, for it was not until after the United States marine laws of 1911 were passed that marine lanterns, with the exception of deck lanterns, required Fresnel lenses. Post-1910 marine lanterns were, for the most part, utilitarian and functional, losing much of the ornate design found on earlier versions.

As a general rule, early pressurized-fuel lanterns can be identified by the absence of a pump in their font, and the absence of a loop in their generator tube. These designs, although carried forward in time by some manufacturers, were dropped by most in favor of a built-in pump and a looped generator tube. There are many designs for pressurized-fuel lanterns. Again, I suggest you study the illustrations to better understand their appearance, variety and availability.

When looking for the name of the manufacturer or model, search the whole lantern, including the bell, font, body, frame or on the globe or underneath the base. Be cautious in dating a lantern by a patent date stamped on it. Remember that the lantern might have been made over a twenty-year period with the same patent date stamp. Note also that some manufacturers' patent date stamps may refer to only a small part on the lantern (e.g., size of globe plate hole, bail shape, etc.). Thus, a lantern may have been manufactured ten years after the oldest patent date stamped on it, but, for the sake of prestige, the manufacturer kept stamping older patent dates to show, as a kind of advertisement, how many patents applied to it.

Also confusing is the discovery of a patent date on a lantern that is later than the last production date given in the specifications sections in this book. This may indicate that the manufacturer had a large order for a special run of a lantern that was out of production and added a later patent date, applicable to some minor improvement, when the special order was run. Or, it may mean that the manufacturer had a stock of no-longer-produced lanterns that were dug out of mothballs and reworked, with a minor improvement warranting a new patent date, and put back on the market as a reintroduction.

If you find a lantern you cannot date because there is no manufacturer's stamp on it, look up similar-appearing lanterns in this book. This will give you a reasonably accurate date, as manufacturers tended to follow each other's designs. If the lantern and its manufacturer are not noted here, but it has a manufacturer's name and city stamped on it, write to the town clerk or public library there. They may be able to tell you the dates the manufacturer was in business, and thus give you an approximate date for the lantern.

Materials and Finishes

Obviously condition is important to the price of a lantern. To assess condition, you need, among other things, to establish its original material and finish. Where known, I have listed finish specifications in this book.

Manufacturer's shipping records for dead flame, hot-blast and cold-blast lanterns indicate that, apart from special orders, black was the paint color most commonly shipped. There were some exceptions to this, most notably Embury, which shipped its lanterns painted dark green. Many customers, especially the larger users, painted their lanterns a different color after receiving them, often with little care. This painting was done for identification purposes, for there could be several companies operating at one job site — perhaps a water department, highway department, and gas company — and each needed to recognize their own lanterns.

Early marine lanterns were usually made of polished brass or copper, and not painted. After 1910, galvanized steel, a cheaper material, was used for marine lanterns and also was not usually painted. Pressurized-fuel lanterns were manufactured from a number of different metals, including aluminum, steel, copper and brass. Their metal parts can be found chrome plated or nickel plated, or the manufacturer may have painted them, from dulls grays to bright reds.

When you find a painted lantern, whether the paint is original or added after shipping, you need to know if it is covering a copper font, brass top, etc., which could make the lantern more valuable. Always carry a small magnet with you to test painted lanterns you are possibly interested in buying. Some metals will react to the magnet and some will not. You can determine whether there is copper, brass, or steel under the paint because the magnet will not adhere to copper or brass as it does to steel, tin or other metals with high ferrous content. Nickel-plated brass and copper can also be detected in this way.

In general, be cautious and do your homework. You may need to measure, check markings and styles, evaluate finishes and materials, compare it to similar lanterns, and check minor distinguishing features noted in this book, in order to pin down a lantern's identity.

Physical Condition

Value of a lantern is also influenced by physical condition. You might want it, no matter what shape it is in, if it is rare or a model you have specifically been looking for. But the worse the condition, the more it affects the price. Check out the metal for dents, cracks, and rust, especially around the base of the font. Be thorough. Avoid buying a lantern that is so rusted through that you cannot paint or restore it. Check whether the glass globe has any cracks, and whether it fits correctly into the lantern's globe plate. If it does not, it may be the wrong size of globe. Check the illustrations in this book to make sure the globe is the right shape. (Many globes are substitutions from other lanterns.) Does the illustration indicate a hood, or reflector, or mounting clamp that is not there now? These are the things most often missing, especially glass reflectors. Are there any obviously broken parts? A side tube, a ratchet, etc.? Are they fixable?

Some lanterns have been electrified. As long as no hole has been drilled into the lantern — for example, to gain access for a wire through the font, or to add an off/on switch — the value has not been substantially reduced. If one has been drilled, unless it is a very rare lantern, do not buy it. Remember, also, that any lantern that has been electrified is now lacking its burner assembly, an integral, original part.

Pricing

People who consult me about the price of a lantern usually want to know what it cost originally, and what it is worth today. The price of any lantern could vary over the years it was being manufactured. (As I've noted for the common Dietz No. 2 Tubular, it originally sold, in 1876, for $2.47. By 1881 it cost 78 cents; in 1888, 66 cents; and as late as 1950, over $5.00.) Marine lanterns were by far the most expensive. (In 1916, Perkins was selling many of its marine lanterns for $50 to $100 each.) In this book, I have indicated manufacturer's prices — where I know them — along with the specification information for the lantern.

Lantern prices continue to rise as the number of collectors increases. They, of course, are looking for the rarer lanterns, a tendency which drives prices higher. And, as noted before, this trend will continue. Each lantern pictured in this book is rated according to one of the price ranges given below. A specific lantern you are interested in may be illustrated in this or my other volume. But whether or not you find an example of it here, it will be helpful to you to study the lantern ratings of the many illustrations. A general familiarity with the kinds of lanterns that are in each price range will be an asset as you search for additions to your collection.

The prices noted below are not "firm," since they vary according to location, condition, and market demand. But they will give you a reasonable idea of what to expect in pricing over the next few years. These prices assume that the lantern is in fairly good condition, and apply to dead flame, hot-blast and cold-blast lanterns, as well as pressurized-fuel lanterns and marine lanterns made of galvanized steel. These prices supercede the prices given in my first book, as they reflect the changes in the market in a few short years.

Very Common	$20.00 to $55.00
Common	$55.00 to $100.00
Rare	$100.00 to $300.00
Very Rare	$300.00 to $700.00

Very ornate marine lanterns made of copper or brass are higher-priced, even if not in very good condition:

Rare $200.00 to $700.00

Very Rare $500.00 to $900.00 or more.

Keep in mind also these specific characteristics, which make most lanterns rarer and therefore at the high end of their price range:

- Brass or copper; the latter being rarer.

- Silver or gold; silver plated or gold plated.

- Lanterns made prior to 1890.

- Globe color: blue, green and amber are rarest; clear and red, common.

- Globe professionally etched with owner's name.

- Intact color disk inside fire lanterns.

- Glass font lantern in pristine condition.

Appendix A
Dietz Lanterns

Corrections or Additional Information to Book One

1. Page 67.   Some Victor lanterns pre-dating 1910 have been seen. These have flat-top fonts and were probably from the Steam Gauge & Lantern Company buy out by Dietz in 1897.

2. Pages 92, 93.   Fire lanterns, all types: the wind breaks can be found stamped with the date "Jan 1 – 89" on them.

3. Page 93.   The King and Queen lanterns marked "Jan 1 – 89" have wind breaks from the 1888 – 1912 Tubular Fire Department lantern.

4. Page 98.   The Improved Steel Clad lantern can be found with a large square font, marked "8 Day" or "8 Day Burning." These were for highway use.

5. Page 107.   The Boy Brass Safety lantern was also marked "Scout" from 1904 to 1914.

6. Page 114.   Late production Junior Dash lanterns, and all Side or Wagon lamps, can be found with Little Wizard fonts.

Fire Department Lantern
1883 – 1888

Height: 14".
No. 1 burner, 5/8" wick.
Finish: tin, nickel plated; tin,
with nickel-plated copper font.
Hot blast.

Very rare.

Square Tube Fire Lantern
1894 – 1901

No. 1 burner, 5/8" wick.
Finish: all brass, polished; all brass,
nickel plated.
Hot blast.

This lantern preceded the "Queen"
lantern on page 93. Some of these
lanterns are marked "Fire Dept."
on the font.

Very rare.

Fire Department Lantern
1916 – 1940

No. 1 burner, 5/8" wick.
Finish: polished brass; brass, nickel plated.
Cold blast.

A high quality lantern. The main buyer
of these was the manufacturer of La
France fire engines.

Rare.

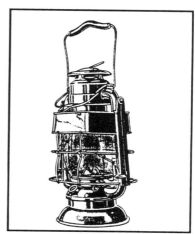

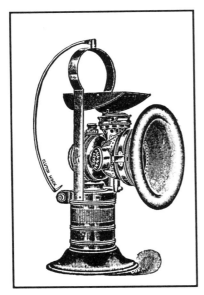

Acetylene Fireman's Lantern
Circa 1930's

Height: 14"; weight, 38 oz.
Finish: all brass, with aluminum reflectors.
6" front reflector.
Cold blast.

Special swivel hook attached to handle, so lantern could be hung from beams, rocks, trees, etc. Had shield to protect hand from lantern heat.

Although it was available through their sales department, it is unlikely that Dietz manufactured this, as they sold no other acetylene lanterns.

Very rare.

Dark Lantern
1917 – 1918

Font: clip-in Sangster, installed from base of lantern; burner: marked "Simplex" and "E. Miller Co."
Globe: clear with unusual straight ribs molded into the glass on the sides.
Their function was to guide a shield that slid up and down to hide the light.
Finish: all brass.
Dead flame.

Can be found with or without the brass tie-down rings mounted on the base. Without the shield, it was called the World Standard Deck Lantern. Both lanterns can be found marked "Dietz" in the center of the top. Very well-made, sturdy construction.

Both were a special order from Perkins Marine Company, who shipped them to the United States Navy during the First World War. A limited number were sold to the public.

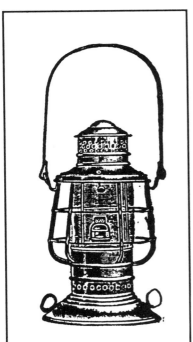

Rare: marked "Dietz."

Very rare: with tie-down rings on side; or not marked "Dietz."

Scout Lantern
1919 – 1928

Sport Lantern
1928 – 1940

Height: 8".
Kerosene burner.
Globe: clear glass made specially for this lantern and marked "Dietz Scout NY USA" or "Dietz Sport NY USA."
Finish: tin, brass or copper. The tin finish appears to have been the most common, followed by brass; copper finish was limited production.

The Scout and Sport lanterns were identical, but marked " Scout" on early versions and "Sport" on later production.

Presenting an identical lantern with two different names was a sales ploy, to appeal to different markets.

Common: tin.

Rare: brass.

Very rare: copper.

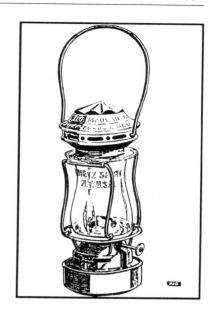

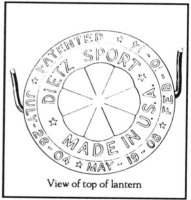

View of top of lantern

Appendix B:
Newell Burner

The Newell burner was specifically designed to be used with camphine lanterns.

Liquid camphine was a very volatile lamp fuel, subject to exploding or at the very least, bursting into flame with careless movement of the lamp. Because of the instability of this fuel, it was customary to use it only on stationary table lamps. Therefore, outdoor portable lanterns using camphine were very rare. In my first volume I included a sketch of a camphine burner, as I had not yet located a photograph. The very rare lantern shown below used a camphine burner.

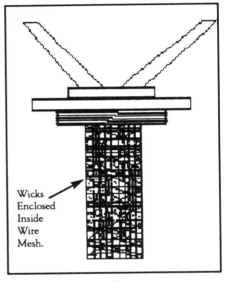

Wicks Enclosed Inside Wire Mesh.

Newell Burner

Well manufactured and in fine condition, its burner is marked "J.NEWELL PATENT OCT. 4 1853." The fact that this lantern still exists almost guarantees it was never used.

The patent issued to Newell was for an improved burner that had a wire mesh screen — silver plated to prevent corrosion — which was suspended into the font between the fuel and the wick. It worked on the principle, discovered in 1816 by Sir Humphrey Davy, that a flame will not pass through a fine wire screen. The patent also included something now

common on all fuel lanterns — a small vent hole in the filler cap to prevent pressure build-up in the font.

Glossary

Acetylene A flammable gas.

Atomization Reducing any liquid to a spray or mist.

Bail A wire handle.

Bell A lantern top.

Bow The forward section of a ship.

Brass An alloy of zinc and copper.

Bronzed Coated with an alloy of copper and tin which gave a yellow to olive-brown color.

Bull's-eye A thick circular piece of glass.

Buoy A float moored on water as a channel or danger marker.

Candlepower Luminous intensity, a measure of brightness.

Canopy A lantern top.

Char The burned area of a wick.

Chromium Decorative plating applied to metal to resist tarnish and rust.

Copper A reddish-brown metal.

Corrugated Glass or metal molded into alternating ridges and grooves.

Crimped Metal pressed into small folds or ridges to provide stiffness and strength.

Dash The panels on the side or front of a carriage or automobile.

Dome A lantern top.

Font The oil reservoir.

Fresnel A lens made in such a way as to amplify and focus light more strongly.

Galvanized A zinc coating applied to steel.

Generator Any apparatus that produces vapor or gas from a liquid.

Girandole A fancy candle holder.

Globe A glass protective covering over the flame.

Government globe A lantern made to government — usually federal — specifications.

Guard A wire encircling the globe to protect the globe from breaking.

Hindi A language of northern India.

Japan A type of enamel or lacquer paint finish originating in the orient.

Lens A molded glass.

Mica Mineral silicate found in rocks and split into thin sheets.

Mild steel A soft, malleable metal.

Nickel-plate An even layer of nickel deposited on metal surfaces by dipping or electroless plating.

Patent date The date of a grant issued by the government to an inventor assuring him the sole right to make, use, and sell his invention.

Port Left side of a ship when you are facing forward.

Re-dipped After lantern was assembled the completed lantern was dipped in a molten tin-lead mixture to recoat all surfaces as an added protection against corrosion.

Rigid fiber bail Bail was locked in the up position. Fiber was insulation for use in electric rail areas.

Sangster A type of locking clip attached to fonts; used on a variety of dead-flame lanterns.

Semaphore A visual signaling light or flag.

Spun metal A mechanical process that gave a smooth shine to the metal.

Starboard Right side of a ship when you are facing forward.

Stem Bow or prow of a ship.

Stern Rear part of a ship.

Streamline The style name given to many lanterns manufactured post 1920s by a process of molding and crimping rather than hand soldering the parts together.

Vapor A cloud or mist.

Bibliography

America's Successful Men of Affairs, An Encyclopedia of Contemporaneous Biography. New York: New York Tribune, 1896.

Black, Linda Lee Young. *Lantern Enlightenment.* Privately published, 1982.

"Book of Michigan Industry." Michigan Manufacturer and Financial Record. April 1945.

Clouett, Bruce and Roth, Matthew. *Bristol, Connecticut, A Bicentennial History 1785-1985.* Canaan, N.H.: Phoenix, 1984.

Coleman Company. *Coleman Lite;* and various Coleman newsletters and pamphlets. Wichita: Coleman Company, 1986 to 1990.

Detroit in History and Commerce. Detroit: Rogers and Thorpe, 1891.

Detroit of Today, The City of Strait, Its Growth, Resources, Commerce, Manufacturing Concerns, Financial Institutions and Prospects. Detroit and Chicago: Phoenix, 1893.

Ebendorf, Herbert W. *Gas from Gasoline.* Wichita: Coleman Company, 1982.

Fuchs, Walter M. *When Oil Wells Run Dry.* Dover, N.H.: Industrial Research Service, 1946.

Giddens, Paul H. *The Birth of the Oil Industry.* New York: Macmillan, 1938.

Perko Archives (Miami, Fla.) List of marine product manufacturers, operating circa 1920.

Pioneering in Big Business. New York: Harper, 1955.

Platt-Seward, Editor. *Dictionary of American Bibliography, Volume VIII.* New York: Charles Scribner's Sons, 1935.

Rushlight Club and Wethersfield Historical Society. "And Then There Was Light." The lighting exhibit of the Rushlight Club and the Wethersfield Historical Society, Old Academy Museum, Wethersfield, Connecticut, August 4 to December 1, 1984. Connecticut: Rushlight Club, 1985.

Scientific American. Issues of the late 1800's, from the collection of the New York Public Library.

Sweetser, M. F., Editor. *King's Handbook of the United States.* Buffalo, New York: Moses King, 1896.

United States Trademark Records, 1900 to 1930. From the collection of the New York State Library, Albany, New York.

Williamson, H. and Daum, A. *The American Petroleum Industry. 1950.*

Index of Individual Lanterns Listed By Manufacturers

This index lists individual lanterns which are mentioned and in most cases illustrated in the text. A list of manufacturers, with dates of operation where known, is given on pages 4-7.

Index

A
Aladdin Security Oil, 62
Aladdin lanterns, 54, 172
Aladdin table lamps, 6, 172
Arc Lamp, 137, 170
Argand, Aime, 60

B
binnacle heads, 80
Boston pattern, 84, 116
British regulation, see English regulation
Brush & Denslo oil, 66
burners, types:
  Cosmos, 70, 71, 106;
  German, 75;
  Glass cone, 71;
  Hydrocarbon, 135;
  Minot, 194, 195;
  Moehring, 43, 50;
  Newell, 220;
  Plume & Atwood, 11, 43;
  Simplex, 218;
  Vortex, 71;
  see also individual lantern specifications

C
Casey, John T., 56
Chase, Guy, 163
cold-blast, lantern, design of, 23; see also individual
  lantern specifications
Coleman Museum, xi, 161
Coleman, William Coffin, 137, 153, 175
condition, 211, 212

D
dead-flame lanterns, see individual lantern specifications

E
Efficient Lamp, 6, 137
enamel, see finishes
English, A. J., 131
English pressurized-fuel (hydrocarbon)
  vapor lamp, 131, 134
English regulation ship lighting, 74, 105;
  see also individual lantern specifications

F
finishes, 210, 211; see also individual lantern
  specifications
Fresnel, August, 69
Fresnel lens, see individual lantern specifications
fuels, types:
  acetylene, 131;
  benzene, 194;

benzol, 194;
butane gas, 201, 202;
camphine, 220;
electric, 131; gasoline, 131;
kerosene, 131;
liquid petroleum, 201;
paraffin, 194;
petroleum derivatives, 142;
propane, 202;
vaclite, 94, 95;
see also individual lantern specifications

G
gas-pressure lantern, see pressurized-fuel lantern
gas-vapor lantern, see pressurized-fuel lantern
generators, development and design of, 142, 143
generators, types:
  O77, 185;
  Q99, 185; R55, 186;
  T44G, 191;
  T66, 187, 188;
  central, 144, 145;
  looped, 143;
  roto-type, 189;
  see also individual lantern specifications

H
Hanson, Hans Christian, 146, 147
Hanson, Russell, 147
hollow wire lighting systems, 143, 144, 153, 155, 156,
  161, 163, 179
hot-blast lantern design, see individual lantern
  specifications

I
Impervious Safety Oil, 64
Instant Lighting, 143
Irby, W. H., 136, 137
Irby-Gilliland lamp, 176-178
Irby vapor lamp, 136, 137, 155, 176

J
japan, see finishes, glossary; see also, individual lantern
  specifications

K
Kitson, Arthur, 131
Kitson vapor-burning lamp, 131, 133, 135

L
LaFrance fire engines, 217
lantern design, changes in, see individual lantern
  specifications

CHICAGO'S RAILROADS AND PARMELEE'S TRANSFER COMPANY:
A Century of Travel.

By Robert D. Parmelee.

Using rare 19th and 20th century photographs, line drawings and maps with its text, this book recreates the story of the advent, growth and eventual decline of Chicago's passenger railroads and their century-long mutual relationship with the Parmelee Transfer Company as, together, they moved millions of immigrants, settlers, business travelers, soldiers and their families, tourists and even corpses. Because each railroad wanted its own station, no passenger or luggage could go through Chicago without changing depots. As a result, for over one-hundred years (1853-1955) – through the opening and settling of the West, commercial and tourism booms, wars and world's fairs – the varied passengers and their mountains of baggage were carried by at least two different railroads and transferred from one station to another by The Parmelee Company. Over 150 illustrations, from fifty private collections and museums, evoke the scenes of these times.

160 pp., 150 B&W illustrations, index.
ISBN 1-889029-03-3. Paperback, 8.5" x 11". $19.95.
ISBN 1-889029-01-7. Hardcover, 8.5" x 11", limited ed., signed, $49.95.

Other Golden Hill Press Titles

HOUSE HISTORIES:
A guide to Tracing the Genealogy of Your Home.

By Sally Light.

Recommended by the American Library Association

This award-winning book explains how to identify the various clues a house may give about its past. Also discussed in detail are the many other possible sources of information — surveys, deeds, wills, censuses, photographs, newspapers, insurance and church records, tax lists, oral interviews, etc. – and how to use them. To help in deciphering such information, an entire chapter deals with reading old handwriting. The book also explains how to apply for a historic register listing and, for those interested in house histories as an occupation, provides several chapters on operating such a business. Doing a house history can be not only fun but rewarding, since it offers the owner, seller or buyer the possibility of increasing the house's value by documenting its origins. A valuable resource for homeowners, preservationists, historians, genealogists, residential real estate brokers and others who deal with old houses.

Preservation League of New York State. "...a good, practical guide to dating and documenting a house through physical inspection and research."

Bangor (Maine) Daily News. "...a book for all home libraries..."

Dallas (Texas) Morning News. "*House Histories*...is a valuable resource..."

Spokane (Washington) Spokesman Review. "Among the unexpected topics touched upon are the nuances of 18th and 19th century American handwriting."

Lincoln (Nebraska) Sunday Journal. "...out-of-the-ordinary."

301 pp., 77+ illustrations, resource section for every state, appendices, glossary, bibliography. ISBN 0-9614876-1-5. Paperback, 6" x 9". $14.95.

HOUSE INSPECTION:
A Homebuyer's/Homeowner's Guide
With a Special Section on Older or Historic Homes.

By Ned Depew.

This book helps the homebuyer/homeowner avoid the frustration of making costly or uninformed decisions. Homebuyers can use this guide to spot problems before negotiating price. And, it can help in evaluating how well a house might fit the buyer's needs. Homeowners/homesellers can use the book to survey and evaluate even minor problems which might put off potential buyers. Taking you step by step through a house and its electrical, plumbing, heating/cooling and structural systems, and floor by floor, from basement to attic, the book details what to look for and what to look at. Easy-to-read check sheets are provided for each area of the house, enabling you to quickly note questions and problems and their locations. Further reference to the text and illustrations will suggest what you should be concerned with and its relative expense, what can be ignored, and when you should seek an outside, professional opinion.

210 pp., 25 B&W drawings, glossary, index.
ISBN 0-6914876-4-X. Paperback, 6" x 9". $11.95.

Available at your local bookstore or from Golden Hill Press, Inc.
Box 122 • Spencertown, New York 12165 • 800/205-0523
When ordering, please add $1.85 postage and handling for the first book
and $.50 for each additional. New York State residents add 8% sales tax.